"*Lean for the Long Term* is one of the only books which presents Lean as comprehensive business model and not just a set of tools in a tool box. An engaging read that will help any company maximize its full business potential, it is a must-read for Business Leaders, C-Suite Executives, and Board Members."

Luke Faulstick
Co-Owner, President and CEO, PPI

"Despite indisputable potential to transform any organization to Great, most Lean transformations fail to get companies to their true potential. Even fewer are able to sustain world-class performance and continuing improvement for the long term. What we know beyond a shadow of a doubt is that Leadership matters, and it really matters to Lean movements. Baker and Rolfes take the reader through myriad thoughtful analyses and recommendations on how to successfully transform an organization and its leadership, and keep it on a perpetual cycle of improvement."

Dan McDonnell
VP, Integrated Supply Chain, Ingersoll Rand

"This work can answer many of the stories of failed Lean implementation. Finally we see a book making the connection between what sometimes look to be two different worlds in the business environment, the executives/strategy and execution/tactics. This is a topic that has not been openly discussed but is definitely a vital one for the long run. A must-read for Lean practitioners, executives, and board members interested in how to address the differences in approach to set the foundation for a sustained Lean business implementation and create value in their businesses."

Mauro G. Gonzalez
Sr. Operations Manager, Littelfuse Inc.

"Lean for the Long Term goes beyond the existing literature on Lean tools and philosophy to describe how to create a Lean transformation that is sustainable across the entire organization for the long haul. Of particular note are the discussions on why transformations fail, and implementation strategies from a variety of perspectives, such as CEO, board member, and Lean practitioner."

Kevin Meyer
Co-Founder of Gemba Academy

A fine review of our Lean journey seen through the eyes of two execs who lived it. Together they cover the operating fundamentals supporting Lean, as well as great illustrations from Lean pioneers.

Patricia E. Moody
Author, Manufacturing and Supply Management Consultant,
The Mill Girl at Blue Heron Journal

This book offers valuable insight to using Lean as a management strategy where it can create a value culture that customers are willing to pay for. Lean is about honoring people, customers, and processes. This book is a must-have for anyone wanting to drive an organization through performance.

Dale Crownover
President /CEO
Texas Nameplate Company
Two-Time Malcolm Baldrige National Quality Award Winner

Lean
FOR THE
Long Term

SUSTAINMENT IS A MYTH, TRANSFORMATION IS REALITY

William H. Baker, Jr. • Kenneth D. Rolfes

CRC Press
Taylor & Francis Group
Boca Raton London New York

CRC Press is an imprint of the
Taylor & Francis Group, an **informa** business

A PRODUCTIVITY PRESS BOOK

CRC Press
Taylor & Francis Group
6000 Broken Sound Parkway NW, Suite 300
Boca Raton, FL 33487-2742

© 2015 by Taylor & Francis Group, LLC
CRC Press is an imprint of Taylor & Francis Group, an Informa business

No claim to original U.S. Government works

Printed on acid-free paper
Version Date: 20141017

International Standard Book Number-13: 978-1-4822-5716-8 (Paperback)

Library of Congress Cataloging-in-Publication Data

Baker, William H., Jr.
 Lean for the long term : maintaining a continuous improvement culture after a management change / William H. Baker, Jr. and Kenneth D. Rolfes.
  pages cm
 Includes bibliographical references and index.
 ISBN 978-1-4822-5716-8 (paperback)
 1. Organizational effectiveness. 2. Organizational change. 3. Total quality management. 4. Cost control. 5. Industrial management. I. Rolfes, Kenneth D. II. Title.

HD58.9.B3434 2015
658.4′06--dc23   2014039867

Visit the Taylor & Francis Web site at
http://www.taylorandfrancis.com

and the CRC Press Web site at
http://www.crcpress.com

Contents

Preface

What is this book about and how can you use it to your benefit?

Our main focus is to help you and your organization migrate from one kind of management approach to one that more effectively addresses today's problems and equips your enterprise with capabilities for building greater competitive strength. Traditional organizations are slow to react to business changes. They do not engage or inspire people, and they do not show respect for people.

We seek to provide you with the information and understanding you need to help your organization move from a departmentalized, job-oriented, silo-infested work environment to a horizontal line-of-sight, customer-focused behavior we call a Lean management system.

We leave the discussion about Lean tools to others, instead focusing on making Lean matter. Too many organizations fail to achieve or recognize the long-term, great accomplishments enabled through Lean. You'll discover how Lean can yield significant, sustainable performance gains.

Our suggestions for achieving dramatic improvement are based upon living research. We have been involved in the study and application of Lean for more than 30 years, inside and outside many organizations that strive to achieve enterprise excellence and competitive advantage. Many companies that achieve some competitive advantage for the short term do so without venturing into Lean at all. Others that utilize Lean tools have not become Lean, but are just doing Lean stuff. In fact, most manufacturers are doing Lean stuff today. Lots of techniques, programs of the month, tactics, and strategies have been tried. Most do not get a significant return on their investment because doing Lean stuff is not the same as becoming Lean.

Becoming Lean requires first a common language of business to be able to communicate, which the Lean community seems to delight in avoiding. Obscure Japanese terms that are everyday language in Japan are not familiar in English or other languages. Business professionals are not necessarily wowed by obscure terms. What gets their attention are sales, cash flow, margins and profits, and profitable growth and it should be everybody's business. We suggest everyone learn the financial fundamentals of business in Chapter 1 and become knowledgeable of the company's performance and how it compares to the best in their industry.

We propose a Lean management system model that encompasses leadership, process, and growth as the model to drive business performance. The core management model has five elements, Clarity of Purpose, Standard Work, Transparency, Accountability, and Innovation. This management system is not your production improvement program; it is the system across the organization. Figure 0.1 illustrates how the tools are applicable across the organization; however, as we stated previously we are not about the tools but about Lean management and leadership. While the elements may sound easy, they require discipline to apply and have less impact if focused solely on operations. We illustrate several companies that have applied the model with outstanding success. However, what this means is our Lean practitioners need to raise their game and become focused on the business model that the company employs to deliver customer value and the culture that supports the value delivery.

Company Strategy	Sales & Marketing	Quality	Production	Supply Chain	Product Development	People	Support Operations	Plant Strategy
Business Strategy	VOC	Quality at the Source	5S	Demand Pull Scheduling	Lean Project Management	Involvement	Gemba	Cellular Manufacturing
Operations Strategy	Business Value Mapping	Poka Yoke	Pull Systems	Heijunka	VOC	Kaizen Improvement	Leader Standard Work	Process flow
Organization Change Strategy	S & OP	Six Sigma	Cell Design	FIFO	Platform Designs	TWI/JI	TPM	Flexible Manufacturing
Strategic Framework	Visual Controls	Structured Problem Solving	Kanban	Kanban Material Withdraw	DFM	Cross Functional Skill Development	Kaizen Blitz	Group Technology
VSM Mapping	Standard Work	Visual Controls	Andon	VMI	10 × 10 × 10	Multi-Functional Workers	Lean Office	Lean Energy
A3	Flow	FMEA	SMED	Small/One Unit Batch Sizes	3P Methodology	Line-of-Sight Management	Autonomation	Ergonomics
			Visual Controls	Point of use Storage		Teamwork	Digitized Information Processes	Green
			Line Balancing					
			Takt Time					
			Process Wheel					

It's Not about the Tools

Figure 0.1 Lean enterprise tools.

The inspiration for this book was observing companies that have made great progress with Lean transformations and with leadership change lost interest. And leaders change regularly. The average tenure of a departing CEO has declined from approximately 10 years in 2000 to 8.1 years in 2012. This means in the S&P 500 there is an average of 63 leadership changes per year. Maintaining a customer-focused Lean strategy and continuous improvement culture can become a challenge when management changes often, unless it has become an institutionalized company-branded business management system. Companies such as Danaher with their Danaher Business System, which stayed the course over 25 years and profited handsomely through three CEO changes, are rare.

What you will find in the book are several company approaches to successful transformation that translated to becoming Lean for the long term and the results that they have achieved. They have been successful because they have been diligent and been able to adopt and adapt a Lean culture and management system across the enterprise, in all departments, functions, and divisions, as we have seen in Danaher, Toyota, Autoliv, and others. The main goal is not to be Lean, but to be successful and achieve excellence for the long term. We believe Lean strategy is the best way to achieve this level of success! However, a Lean strategy is more than continuous improvement programs and Kaizens. Innovation requires a business to continually challenge its business model, product offerings, and technology in order to survive. We suggest there is no such thing as sustainment unless you're dead. A Lean management system is designed to build a culture of constant transformation; otherwise, the company becomes antiquated and obsolete. After all, of the original S&P 500 company list in 1957, only 65 companies remain on it. Extinction is an option.

If you want to skip through the book to address the topic from your vantage point, look at the chapter titles. If you are a board member, for example, read the chapter "What the Board Should Know about Lean." If you are CEO, senior manager, or Lean practitioner, you should find a chapter that speaks to you. In a Lean organization, everyone is a leader and has a vital role to play in Lean for the long term and the viability of the business.

For every reader, we suggest you use Chapter 9 as a guide and encouragement to build your own action plan based on those best practices we have highlighted. The focus here is almost entirely on leadership aspects of Lean and the management systems. After all, as Peter Drucker described, management is the distinctive organ of all organizations.

Up until now, there have been few, if any, in-depth discussions on Lean as a strategy and management system. We hope you enjoy the book and find it inspiring to move toward a broader, more strategic use of Lean principles in your business. If you wish to contribute your thoughts, we would enjoy hearing from you.

Introduction

Description of *Lean for the Long Term*

Lean for the Long Term levels an unflinching look at today's organizations that are applying Lean tools in their operations, the rhetoric around the wonderful results achieved, and the reality of how most companies fall short. While being "Customer Focused" is widely used in companies today, the departmentalized, job-oriented, silo-infested work environment inhibits organizations from understanding their customers and acting in their own self-interest. Authors Baker and Rolfes assert that the Lean tools focus and the management systems employed by traditional organizations are too slow to react to business changes that make them vulnerable to obsolescence. You are probably a successful CEO, Executive, or Lean practitioner. You may even be one of the best.

Lean for the Long Term can help you be better.

Better in that you will stop thinking about Lean in terms of consultants, limited benchmarking and the next new tool you should be learning. It will help you to focus more on how to use Lean to make your organization faster, more flexible, and customer focused. Better in that you will stop forcing new Lean language on people who look at it with suspicion, and communicate with the universal language of business. Better in that you will stop compartmentalizing improvement efforts and use a less complex Lean management system to guide all organizational actions. Better in that you will stop thinking in terms of sustaining, and more in terms of continually transforming and growing your business for the future.

Lean for the Long Term demonstrates with examples from companies who have adopted Lean as a management system to drive superior performance for their people, customers and investors over a number of years. It offers:

- Insights in how to use the language of business to communicate and set objectives
- Profiles of management systems employed by leading companies such as Danaher, Hillenbrand, Ford, Autoliv, and others
- Roles and action guidelines for Lean leaders at all levels of the organization from the Lean Practitioner, Executive, CEO and Board of Director
- Approaches how to create a horizontal line-of-sight, customer-focused behavior that we call a Lean management system

Chapter 1

Total Business Thinking Required

Let's cut to the chase. For the limited approach that most companies have attempted to become Lean, the results are questionable. While Lean proponents tout the benefits and many companies claim they are doing Lean, for most the impact is inconsequential. We all know that we have to be fast, we have to be agile. So, are Lean methodologies ineffective? Quite the contrary, they are profoundly impactful. The barrier is our traditional organizational management systems prevent Lean from being adopted correctly and broadly enough in a business to have an effect. Consequently most companies have not shown significant impact on their business models, financials, or management systems.

Lean seems to be dependent on leaders who can talk the language and understand the impact Lean can make in the business. Lean practitioners schooled in the methodologies and tools thrive under Lean savvy leaders and struggle when there are leadership shifts. Financial managers find it difficult to see how Lean is helping the business performance. CEOs and other senior managers outside of manufacturing consider Lean to be on someone else's to-do list. Learning the Lean language is not something many wish to take the time out of their busy day to become comfortable with. Finally few, including Lean practitioners, realize the growth and profitability performance that Lean business strategies and management systems can deliver over the long term. As a result Lean activities or methodologies continue to be limited to a small part of the organization, limiting the impact Lean can make to a business.

Since the 2009 great recession we are living in a low-growth world which has an overcapacity of most everything, (except possibly common sense, but we won't divert into that tangent). Products become commodities overnight and technologies frequently disrupt companies into nonexistence. Our premise is that in today's world of rapid-changing economic, political, technological, and demographic environment, the flexibility of Lean business systems are more capable of surviving and prospering than the management systems built around highly structured departmental organizational goals, resourcing plans, and controls.

Lean is a customer centric business model and a management system to support the model. It requires that business leadership come from all levels of the organization and the leaders understand the business model in which the organization operates. It is dependent upon the leaders at all levels to be able to communicate in the same language and view their role more holistically within the business model they are operating. And language needs to be a universal language of business.

Is a Poka-Yoke something we would see on *Dancing with the Stars*?* When we do Kaizens, do we want people to think "outside the box" while remaining "on the same page"? When we schedule using Heijunka, are we "throwing it over the wall"? When we "take it offline," am I going to Gemba? Is a "mindshare" a "brain dump"? Can you achieve "synergy" by using a "holistic approach," or do we just get Jishu Hozen? What the heck? Despite the relentless attack on their use by the comic strip Dilbert and other enemies of corporate gobbledygook, buzzwords continue to prosper on the manufacturing floor, cubicles, offices, and boardrooms. One might observe that our companies are simply a manifestation of the modern-day Tower of Babel if it were not for our fearless leaders.

Jim Collins in his studies of companies since 1996 found that great companies are highly dependent upon the leader. Great companies, we have learned, have a solid understanding of what business the company is in. Unfortunately, many don't and make mistakes, sometimes big mistakes. Consider GM; Alfred Sloan has been quoted in articles and books as saying, "GM is in the business of making money, not motorcars." At one time, General Motors was considered the preeminent U.S. corporation, a giant among giants, but in 2008 it was bankrupt after years of losing market share.

---

* Dancing with the Stars is the popular television show that features well-known personalities attempting complex dance steps.

That compares with a market cap of about $56 billion in 2000, when the stock was at its all-time high of $94.62 a share.

GM has since gotten back on its feet, with government help, to recover its market cap at around $56 billion as of this writing. Also at this writing, GM has made headlines with a total of 60 recalls, covering almost 30 million vehicles. What began earlier in 2014 with an ignition switch, recalls have swelled in numbers, congressional hearings, and company scapegoating. "General Motors engineers knew 10 years ago about a problem with ignition switches in some of its most popular models, but it took until recently to issue a recall. By that time, there had been at least 13 deaths as a result of the issue."[*] The current General Motors Co. chief executive, Mary Barra, was prodded by Capitol Hill lawmakers on why it took so long to recall the defective vehicles. It has been reported that GM managers ruled out redesigning the flawed ignition switch because the fix would have added $0.90 to a car, and savings would only be 10 to 15 cents in returns warranties. "In the past," Ms. Barra told them, "we had more of a cost culture, and now we have a customer culture that focuses on safety and quality."[†] Apparently Alfred Sloan's definition of the business GM is in has persisted.

Alfred Sloan was also instrumental in the development of modern management theory. Peter Drucker credited the no-nonsense executive with being the designer and architect of management and first to work out systematic organization in a big company. Sloan viewed management as a science which included planning, strategy, measurements, and the principle of decentralization into departments.[‡] This gave rise to managing by objectives (MBOs) and managing diverse operations with financial statistics. As a result, most people work in departments frequently isolated from other departments, working to their own goals and far from the customer the business is supposed to be serving. Few have the opportunity to see the total business, much less the customer.

In the meantime, a little company with limited resources called Toyota, which was struggling to survive and grow after World War II, took a different approach with its Toyota Production System, which we call Lean today. Toyota turned necessity into virtue, coming up with a system to focus its organization on customers and get as much as possible out of the limited resources that it had available—every part, every machine, and every worker. The principles are simple, perhaps obvious—understand the value

---

[*] *CNN Money*, February 28, 2014.
[†] GM's Troubled Legacy Weighs on CEO in Capitol Hill Grilling, *Wall Street Journal*, April 2, 2014, p. 1.
[‡] Rick Wartzman, Lessons from the Alfred Sloan Era, *BusinessWeek*, June 12, 2009.

customers want, make what is ordered by customers in the quickest and most efficient way, in order to deliver as quickly as possible, and then collect payment. Its approach is simple as well: do away with non-value-added waste, make problems visible, and fix them as soon as they arise, and do this continually. The company has, better than any other, turned principle into disciplined practice and engaged its people to maintain its approach. Toyota has also been the company that has made the most profit of any in the automotive industry over the last 25 years.

Most people live, whether physically, intellectually or morally, in a very restricted circle of their potential being. They make very small use of their possible consciousness and of their soul's resources in general, much like a man who, out of his whole bodily organism, should get into a habit of using and moving only his little finger.

—William James, American philosopher and psychologist, leader of the philosophical movement of pragmatism, 1842–1910

Toyota, however, is not without its own problems. A year after the failure of Lehman Brothers Holdings, Inc. and the financial crisis in 2008 sent car demand tumbling, Toyota recalled more than 10 million vehicles to fix problems linked to unintended acceleration, damaging its reputation for quality. In 2014, the company agreed to pay a record $1.2 billion penalty to end a probe by the U.S. Justice Department, which said Toyota had covered up information and misled the public at the time. It has also spent the years after 2008 rebuilding its reputation. The company president, Akio Toyoda, has been quoted as saying he felt Toyota got big company disease, and so he went back to its principles, and also paused from announcing any new car assembly plants. Apparently these efforts have succeeded. When *Consumer Reports* released its 2014 Car-Brand Perception Survey, Toyota achieved top honors as having the best reputation among car owners. Additionally, Toyota's stock price to sales ratio is twice that of GM.

Today we see that Lean production techniques have revolutionized operations. *BusinessWeek*, *Fortune*, and other business publications have gone as far as identifying the Toyota Production System as one of the most significant advances in technology, psychology, and analytics in the 20th century.

Figure 1.1   Dilbert deals with change.

Over the years we have seen Lean tools become more pervasive, to the point that most companies are claiming to be doing "Lean stuff." Lean has also penetrated the healthcare, financial, military, retail services, and other industry sectors.

In spite of this, business strategies and performance metrics seem to shift with each management change and business cycle. In addition, organization bureaucracy reigns and continues to provide material for the humor in Dilbert cartoons (Figure 1.1). Departmental silos, miscommunication, and misaligned goals plague our corporations. We even have departments for continuous improvement. Oh, by the way, why do we have continuous improvement (CI) departments in the first place? Have we really progressed our understanding of becoming a high-performance Lean business, or just created more silo organizations?

Lean has now found its own language. Its buzzwords have become part of our lexicon. Kaizen, value stream maps, Kanbans, 5S, A3s, team boards, and other tools can be found in the vocabulary of most companies we visit these days. Ah, have we cause to celebrate? Not long ago it was hard to find companies doing Lean, much less getting good at it. Consequently, books have proliferated, consultants have multiplied, and tools have been taught. Click on your favorite search engine and in about 0.28 second there are 263 million results covering acronyms and icons for Lean terms and their origins. There are sites for the Lean dictionary. The Lean Enterprise Institute has published the *Lean Lexicon*, a glossary of terms for Lean thinkers. An oxymoron if we ever found one.

Can it be that operations, CI practitioners, and leaders are living in their own world, not connecting with their business and senior leadership? Consider the following exchange: "I can tell you are an engineer," the CEO of the company said as Ken showed him an X matrix and extolled the virtues of Hoshin Kanri strategic planning methodology as a way of aligning the company's vision and priorities across all levels of the organization. Of course, Ken made sure to explain Hoshin Kanri as a strategic planning process to establish a True North Vision and overarching corporate strategy. "I suppose if I were Sir Ernest Henry Shackleton* or Robert Edwin Peary, Sr.† I would be enticed by true north, but this is a business and we need to get down to the business of meeting our plan," was his response. They weren't talking the same language. Ken hadn't connected with the business. Luckily, he was young and had learned a valuable lesson.

Jim Collins in *Good to Great* described a Level 5 leader as one where people are the starting point and strategy second. He also went on to say, "While Level 5 leadership is not the only requirement for transforming a good company into a great one—other factors include getting the right people on the bus (and the wrong people off the bus) and creating a culture of discipline—his research shows it to be essential. Good-to-great transformations don't happen without Level 5 leaders at the helm. They just don't."‡

According to Collins, there are five attributes that typify Level 5 leaders:

1. They are self-confident enough to set up their successors for success.
2. They are humble and modest.
3. They have "unwavering resolve."
4. They display a "workmanlike diligence—more plow horse than show horse."

---

* Sir Ernest Henry Shackleton (February 15, 1874–January 5, 1922) was a polar explorer who led three British expeditions to the Antarctic, and subject of a number of movies about his Arctic adventures and the disastrous expedition to the Antarctic when his ship, *Endurance*, became trapped in pack ice and was slowly crushed before the shore parties could be landed. There followed a sequence of exploits, and an ultimate escape with no loss of human life, that would elevate Shackleton to heroic status.

† Robert Edwin Peary, Sr. (May 6, 1856–February 20, 1920) was an American explorer who claimed to have reached the geographic North Pole with his expedition on April 6, 1909. Peary's claim was widely credited for most of the 20th century, rather than the competing claim by Frederick Cook, who said he got there a year earlier. Both claims were widely debated, however. Modern historians generally think Cook did not reach the pole. Based on an evaluation of Peary's records, current historians conclude that Peary did not reach the pole, although he may have been as close as 5 miles (8 km).

‡ Jim Collins Level 5 Leadership, *Harvard Business Review*, January 2001.

5. They give credit to others for their success and take full responsibility for poor results. They "attribute much of their success to 'good luck' rather than personal greatness."

So, how do you develop these attributes? Collins stated that it would "trivialize the concept" to give a 10-step list to Level 5.

No wonder we continue to see Lean success as highly senior management dependent and fragile, and it comes and goes with changes at the top. And, leadership changes on a regular basis. In the last 10 years almost the entire S&P 500 has turned over the CEO position. Younger players have taken the reins, with 74% of the CEOs as internal candidates. With those younger leaders mostly internally developed for leadership succession, can we expect to see a stronger engagement in Lean? Will they focus on the development of organizations that concentrate their energy on what is truly effective and build a Lean, robust, high-performing company? Well, maybe. It would seem Lean process improvement methods have become more widely adopted in recent years. The MPI Next Generation Manufacturing Study, released in November 2013, showed that nearly 90% of all plants in the United States are currently employing Lean manufacturing tools for process improvement, however few are becoming Lean or world class.

Obviously, senior leadership changes will continue, and to make their companies stronger, they need to create an enterprise where the right people with the right skills are supported by a vibrant organizational structure, processes, and tools. This is the nature of what a Lean culture should be in our companies. The leadership task is to build a Lean robust organizational structure and culture that reflects the company's strategic focus.

When an organization has achieved this level of performance, you can feel it the moment you walk in the door. In high-performing organizations people are energized. They are confident about the strategy and the changes that are occurring rather than simply going through the motions. They know what they are supposed to do and how what they do relates to the tasks of their associates and customers' needs. High-performance organizations also deliver top-line growth and earnings.

Leaders at Every Level

While leadership starts at the top, it does not stop at the top. Organizations have leaders at every level. Middle managers oversee the vast majority of employees, translating the company's mission, vision, and strategy into concrete plans for their teams. Unfortunately, when we talk with operations and continuous improvement leaders, what we find is not really encouraging. Middle managers seem to get lost in the shuffle and receive insufficient support and attention from senior leaders. Given that most improvements are led from the middle, and the middle managers continue to have difficulty engaging senior management in developing a Lean culture, it makes one wonder how long this Lean stuff can be sustained. The improvements being made at times are difficult to relate to business results, and senior management simply cannot connect to daily problems. Yes, having a neat plant develop from a 5S initiative looks good, but how does it relate it to business results? What is happening is that Lean practitioners are doing Lean stuff rather than the company developing a Lean culture or becoming truly Lean.

> As Warren Buffet advises investors, "I try to buy stock in businesses that are so wonderful that an idiot can run them, because sooner or later, one will."

As for communicating with senior management, "I cannot get on the calendar until next month," says one. "We have different departments going in different directions," reports another. "We don't look at the balance sheet as a performance measure," a senior operations VP told me recently. "Margins always win." So, we wait for the Level 5 leader to appear. Maybe operations and CI leaders need to lead the culture from where they are and stop "waiting for Godot."*

As Stanley Bing, the longtime business humorist and columnist for *Fortune*, reminds us, those in the lower ranks need to manage up. "**Managing up**, as he describes, is the art of getting your superiors to do what you want. Those at the top are no less in need of good management than those in the lower branches of the corporate tree. The problem: There's

---

* *Waiting for Godot* is an absurdist play by Samuel Beckett in which two characters, Vladimir and Estragon, wait endlessly and in vain for the arrival of someone named Godot.

nobody around to manage them unless their subordinates do it."* While it may sound career limiting, chances for success increase if real communication can be achieved. This requires leaders at every level to be fluent in the language of business.

The Language Is Important

In the mid-1980s, Ken began his first plant transformation at an operation in decline. At that time there were a few articles in business magazines, including one about the Kawasaki plant in Lincoln, Nebraska, which had Just-in-Time (JIT) in operation and was highlighted in Richard Schonberger's books *Japanese Manufacturing Techniques*, published in 1982, and *World Class Manufacturing*, published in 1986. Otherwise, there were few, if any, companies known to be practicing this Japanese manufacturing methodology.

Ready to try these methods to revitalize a high-mix, relatively low-volume production operation, he charged forward. Communication, he had learned, was critical to success, so we began by describing what was needed for the operation to be successful, to continue to exist, and how the JIT approach would help the operation. The goal was to drive urgency with a clear direction. The response was anything but.

Concerns about layoffs immediately came to the forefront. The initials for Just-in-Time (JIT) became Just-Isn't-There since material shortages were always an issue. And one day a drawing of an interpretation of cellular manufacturing (see Figure 1.2) was posted in the hall.

Mayday! Mayday! The transformation process was going down fast; Ken's approach needed to change. The people (about 350) there were mostly women, and some about the age of his mother. He had told them to call him Ken, as Kenneth was only used by his mother when she was angry and he had to listen up. They picked up on it, and one day a small group of them called him over to their workstations and said, "Kenneth, you are losing us!" Clearly he had to listen. The people needed a better understanding of the purpose of the changes and what was in it for them. Yes, people needed to learn to recognize and eliminate waste. Most importantly, though, the communication had to engage the people so they could see how the waste was robbing the performance of the operation, perhaps their livelihood, and that doing something about it would improve their lives.

---

* Stanley Bing, The New ABCs of Business, *Wall Street Journal*, April 12, 2014, p. C1.

Cellular Manufacturing

Figure 1.2   Cellular manufacturing.

The pressing issue for the plant at the time was customer delivery service, which was spotty at best. The operation was measured on contribution margin, which no one really understood, and process metrics other than scrap costs and variances were nonexistent. On-time delivery was measured by how many calls were received from sales and the management level of the caller. The shift in the communication approach was to make customer experience the driver and focus activities around the customer. Would you continue to go to the same store for milk if half of the time it was out of what you needed? What happens when customers stop coming to the store? This became our burning platform, to use the cliché. Our mantra became: "Let's work on only those activities that satisfy customer orders or keep the desired finished goods stock level." With the boss it was: "We are only going to work on what we get paid for from our customers."

The approach was to convert the plant to a build-to-demand model from the traditional MRP (Material Requirements Planning) forecast-driven work orders. There were too many finished goods part numbers (approximately 8,000) to continue the monthly cycle of master planning. So the plant went from having four planners to a few thousand planners called customers and got everyone out of the way so production could respond to customer needs. People began to grasp the concept, and their experience working in focused product teams (what Lean practitioners call cells) broke down barriers, changed behavior, and shrunk lead time. The sales complaints and expediting calls stopped, with the continuous flow of the right products either going direct to our customers on time or maintaining finished goods stock levels. Later, with experience and production consistency, finished goods turns began to rise.

The business financial metrics and operations driver metrics of customer experience, quality, lead time, and total cost needed to be connected. The initial order-to-completion cycle time was far longer than it needed to be. The typical estimates of 5% of the time is value-add time that the Lean practitioners talk about as the benchmark was far too generous. The production floor was filled with work orders and work-in-process, which the cost accounting system would use for absorption in the contribution margin numbers. Along with educating the plant floor people, it was necessary to educate the bosses in a way that supported the business performance in terms of customer experience, cash flow, and product margins as well. With the work-in-process dropping rapidly, the plant generated a lot of cash, but was not absorbing the overhead, so the contribution margin suffered. Fortunately, Ken's boss understood the plant was in transition and the improvements in customer experience and cash generation saw them through. You can take cash to the bank or spend it; you cannot do that with percentages, and the wisdom of measuring operations on contribution margins came under question. In all of these efforts, linking the language of business and the language of the factory was instrumental to making the change. It was important to become bilingual to succeed.

Learning the Language

Chances are you have built your career in one area of your company such as operations, sales, engineering, finance, or human resources. These areas are vital business functions and probably have their own language, buzzwords, and acronyms. Perhaps your career track has allowed you to move up within the function. Such career tracks tend to narrow your perspective which influence decisions and tradeoffs you make each day. What is best for your department or function may not necessarily be what is best for the whole business or customer the business serves.

Successful business leaders have a way of bringing the most complex businesses down to the fundamentals: the building blocks of business design and operation — Customers, Cash, Margins, Velocity, and Growth. All are positively impacted by a Lean culture and Lean methodologies. Most of all, business leaders see the company as a total business and are expected to make decisions that enhance overall performance.

While many functional managers would rather have a root canal than learn about finance, an understanding of a few financial measures, coupled with a total business perspective, can help them connect with the business model in which their company operates. Understanding the monetary intake of a company, what is driving its growth, cash generation, and return on assets can help counteract the managerial tendency to think only within one's department or unit. When you speak the language of business you can have meaningful discussions with anyone in the company.

Looking at startup companies as well as private and public companies, the fundamentals of business are the same. Experience has shown the importance of three elements that allow you to have influence and real impact in your company. These ingredients are:

■ Command of the business language to have meaningful discussions with senior executives, suppliers, and customers.
■ An understanding of the mission and vision of the company and what makes the company work.
■ Becoming connected and engaged in the business across departments beyond your functional department.

Unfortunately, many operations and continuous improvement people fall short in these areas. Their business language skills and knowledge are weak, which reduces their ability to communicate effectively with senior leaders and, at times, their own staff. Additionally, surveys have found that fewer than 40% of employees know what their company stands for and what makes its brand different from its competitors' brands.* CI and operations management are not immune to this knowledge gap, which weakens their position of influence in their companies. As a result, we see frustrated CI and operations people experts in Lean tools but not the business of the company.

Gallup estimates that companies with disengaged employees experience lower earnings per share (or EPS) than their competition during the same time period. They go further to estimate that active disengagement costs U.S. companies $450 billion to $550 billion per year. For the CI people who may

---

* Gallup, State of the American Workplace 2013, Employee Engagement Insights for U.S. Business Leaders.

be engaged but lack business language and knowledge of their company's business, customers, and goals, their prospects for success and promotion are decreased, which make it impossible to lead from where they are in the organization. Ask yourself, do you speak the language of business, do you understand your company, or are you stuck in "Lean speak"?

There are really two aspects to speaking the language of business. First, you need to have the right focus. Second, you need the right language. The focus of a manager or staff member in a functional department is likely to be on specific tasks, costs, and operational details. Here, the language is that of departmental activity. Upper management of the organization, however, has a completely different focus and language. Their focus is holistic (or should be), including company goals and, in a for-profit company, profit. A company's primary responsibility is to serve its customers. Surprisingly, profit is not the primary goal, but rather an essential condition for the company's continued existence and sustainability.*

Aligning Lean Speak with the Business Speak

Understanding the interrelationships between the firm's major processes and resources required to achieve its objectives and provide value to its customers and shareholders is part of the CEO's job. Their language is the language of business: revenue, cash, margins, velocity, growth, and customers. Every decision made in the process of running a business will eventually make its way to the financial statements. In operations it is no different, however it is the nonfinancial processes that lead to the results, and relating these processes to the firm's performance is the language required to garner attention.

For example, an operations manager wanted to justify to his CEO efforts in 5S and cross-training programs in a company with a seasonal business that rapidly hires temporary workers to handle peak demand. How quickly people can be hired and trained is a critical operational performance factor. A slow ramp-up time would cause too many temporary people on the books for too long, overtime, or delays in meeting demand. All of this can be translated into costs, margins, and revenue impact. It is more than a clean plant and shadow boards.

One can demonstrate the relationship of Lean efforts using an adaptation of the DuPont analysis, which was a method of performance measurement

---

* Peter F. Drucker, *The Practice of Management*, 1954. Harper and Row; New York.

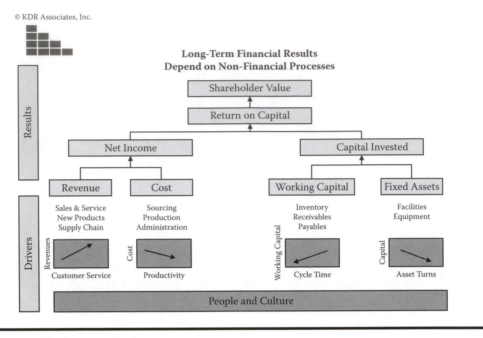

Figure 1.3 DuPont analysis.

started by the DuPont Corporation in the 1920s, shown in Figure 1.3. This analysis tells us that company shareholder value is affected by its return on invested capital (equity and debt), which is derived from two important drivers:

■ Operating efficiency: This is measured by profit margin.
■ Asset use efficiency: This is measured by total asset turnover.

As shown in Figure 1.3, these results come from nonfinancial actions taken to grow revenue, improve productivity, and increase the velocity of the assets applied to achieve the net income of the company. While valuing and comparing new and high-growth companies requires a different approach than those generally used by investors to value and compare more stable and established companies, the model in Figure 1.3 applies to most every business in the long term.

So for simplicity, we can say the language of business is money, since that is the common denominator for measuring, evaluating, and managing various types of business. Decisions are made based on whether the issue in question will increase earnings, cover cost, and sustain future operations. There is simply no other denominator that can effectively track and objectively compare the diverse activities required to make a business work or to compare different businesses.

Bilingual Language of Business

To be successful, therefore, a Lean leader must be bilingual in the language of business. The leader must be able to communicate effectively with supervisors and staff, speaking the language of the functional departmental activity. While most can do this, the Lean leader must also be fluent, comfortable, and confident speaking the language of business to upper management. The business case for investment in improvement initiatives must be aligned with company business needs. Communications must have the right focus and be expressed in the right language of business. Any additional staff or budget must be made in terms of the expected contribution to achieving the organization's goals and, when possible, in terms of the increased revenue, cash, or improved margins expected from the proposed investment. In other words, start from their perspective of what is important and use their language—not from your perspective and certainly not with Lean jargon.

Refer to the results section in Figure 1.3, and answer the following questions about your company:

1. What were the company's sales in the last year? Last quarter?
   Look at the company financials on the P&L in the latest report.
2. Is the company growing, flat, or declining? Is the growth picture good enough?
   Look over the past 3 to 5 years of quarterly results on the P&L. What is the top line doing? Is it growing? Is it growing by its own sales efforts (revenue) or growing by acquiring other businesses, or both? How important are new products to your company's growth? What percent of revenue do new products contribute?
3. What is the company's profit margin? Is it growing, declining, or flat?
   Gross margin: This value measures the percent of revenue left after paying all direct production expenses. It is calculated as revenue minus the cost of goods (COG) sold divided by the revenue and multiplied by 100.
   Look over the past 3 to 5 years of quarterly results. What is the cost of goods sold doing relative to sales? Is it growing or shrinking?
4. How do your company's sales growth and profits compare with competitors'? How do they compare to other relevant industries'? Is the company gaining or losing to competition?
   If your company is public, most brokerage websites can provide you the information on competitors and how your company compares in

performance. Look at Reuters, Standard & Poor's, and other stock analysis reports.

5. What is the company's inventory turns? Its asset turns?

Asset turns is calculated as: Sales ÷ Total assets

Inventory turns can be calculated in two ways:

1. Generally calculated as

$$= \frac{Sales}{Inventory}$$

2. However, inventory turns may also be calculated as

$$= \frac{Cost\ of\ goods\ sold}{Average\ inventory}$$

Sales are annual and inventory is normally the inventory value on the balance sheet at the end of the reporting period.

6. What is the company's return on assets (ROA) or return on capital (debt + equity)?

An indicator of how profitable a company is relative to its total assets. ROA gives an idea as to how efficient management is at using its assets to generate earnings. Calculated by dividing a company's annual earnings by its total assets, ROA is displayed as a percentage. Sometimes this is referred to as return on invested capital (ROIC).

The formula for return on assets is

$$= \frac{Net\ income}{Total\ assets}$$

Return on assets: This value is the income after taxes divided by the total assets on the balance sheet, expressed as a percentage.

Return on capital: This value is the income after taxes divided by the debt plus equity invested in the company.

7. Is your company's cash generation increasing or decreasing? What is driving cash increases or decreases?

Look at the company's cash flow statement. It is a financial statement that shows how changes in balance sheet accounts and income affect cash and cash equivalents, and breaks the analysis down to operating, investing, and financing activities. Look at cash flow over a number of years to see the trend. If you are in operations, look at the cash provided by operating activities.

When you can answer the above questions, you are speaking the language of business and you will be more knowledgeable than most people in the company. Recognize, however, that what we are looking at is the results. At the end of the day, as we all know, companies need to make their numbers as they report to their owners. In the public company environment, and most private equity-owned companies, CEOs are responsible for delivering performance, and they report to the board of directors that represent the interests of the owners. The CEO must work with his or her management team to understand the key metrics in each area that will lead to expected performance. The expectation is that the CEO and his or her management team knows what makes the business work, and can identify and address problem areas before they significantly impact performance. The same expectation should apply to continuous improvement or Lean practitioners. Results are achieved through operating execution, which are tracked in the "Drivers" section in the DuPont model (Figure 1.3). When you can relate your continuous improvement efforts to the above questions, i.e., relate them to the drivers in Figure 1.3, you are talking the language with the right focus. Later, in Chapter 5, we will dive deeper into the DuPont model to illustrate the Lean tools and actions that impact the drivers that deliver business results.

Your Company?

1. Sales: _____

2. Profit: _____

3. Margins: _____

4. Growth: _____

5. Velocity (inventory turns and asset turns): _____

6. Return on assets: _____

7. Cash flow: _____

Chapter 2

How Lean Fails

Much of what we call Lean today has been derived from studies of the Toyota Production System (TPS) and the tools and methodologies associated with it. Today there are as many as 70 tools, and their applications that have been described in books and articles over the past 30 years. Many ask, "Do we just copy Toyota?" The answer is, "Of course you do … if you are Toyota." If not, and most are not Toyota, we need to go back to the principles of Lean, and understand the problems the tools were designed to solve and why Toyota developed the TPS.

Fortunately, the roots of the Toyota Production System are chronicled in a history compiled by the Toyota 75-Year Company History Editorial Committee and also can be found on Toyota's global website.* After World War II, in September 1945, Gen. Douglas MacArthur took charge of the Supreme Command of Allied Powers (SCAP) and began the work of rebuilding Japan. By late 1947 and early 1948, Japan was in an economic crisis, forcing the occupation policies to address the weakening economy. Initiatives in Japan ranged from tax reforms to measures aimed at controlling inflation. The inflation control measures led to a rapid stabilization of prices, but at the same time led to a reduction in the money supply, which plunged industry into a serious shortage of funds, leading to unemployment and a series of business failures.

Businesses in Japan had to find a way to operate in a way to survive and grow during the economic crisis or simply close. The response of Toyota management at the time was to address the most serious needs of improving

---

* For those wishing to read a more complete history, go to www.toyota-global.com/company/history_of_toyota/75years/index.html.

productivity and the effective utilization of materials. Production materials were subject to rationed allocation with officially fixed pricing, while sales were also subject to rationed allocation with officially fixed pricing and distribution by allocation. Toyota found it difficult to cover the difference between the fixed prices of materials and products, so the company operated at a loss. Labor relations were difficult, as job cuts were needed to balance costs and revenues. The only way out, they saw, was increasing efficiency to reduce costs.

Toyota's "autobiography" describes how TPS has evolved through many years of trial and error to improve efficiency based on the Just-in-Time concept developed by Kiichiro Toyoda, the founder (and second president) of Toyota Motor Corporation. The automatic loom invented by Sakichi Toyoda not only automated work, which used to be performed manually, but also built the capability to make quality checks into the machine itself. By eliminating both defective products and the associated wasteful practices, Sakichi succeeded in tremendously improving both productivity and work efficiency.

Kiichiro Toyoda, who inherited this philosophy, set out to realize his belief that "the ideal conditions for making things are created when machines, facilities, and people work together to add value without generating any waste." He conceived methodologies and techniques for eliminating waste between operations, between both lines and processes. As the history describes, the result was the Just-in-Time concept, as well as methods we call Lean tools today.

The post-war period was formative for Toyota, as the company learned how to operate with scarce resources and limited funding. Is it any wonder it was obsessed with the elimination of waste and depended heavily on people? What has set Toyota apart from other companies is that they have stuck with the principles.

TPS Outside of Toyota

Danaher Corporation was an early adopter and is one of the few companies that have been driving performance with its Lean culture for a long time. The company's Danaher Business System (DBS), which is based on Lean strategies pioneered by Toyota Motor Corporation, is widely considered one of the most successful in the industrial sector.

Reviewing Danaher's performance in first quarter 2014, we see the following performance indicators:

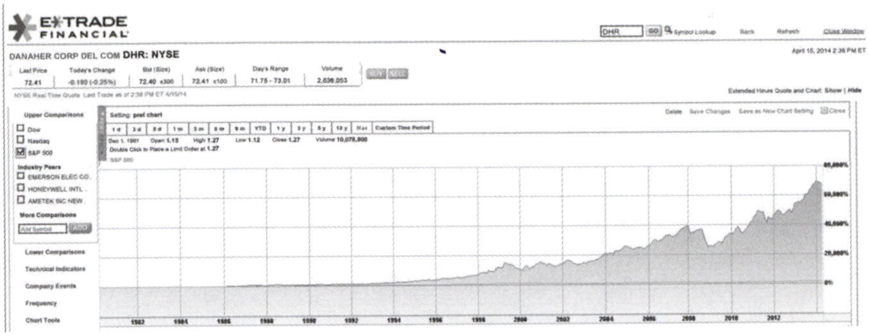

Figure 2.1   Danaher's remarkable performance.

■ The return on equity for Danaher (DHR), for example, shows that it is able to reinvest its earnings more efficiently than 75% of its competitors in the scientific and technical instruments industry. Typically, companies that have higher return on equity values are more attractive to investors.

■ DHR's gross margin is more than 71% of other companies in the scientific and technical instruments industry, which means it has more cash to spend on business operations than its peers. As indicated by the operating margin, DHR controls its costs and expenses better than 92% of its peers.[*]

■ The investor return has been orders of magnitude greater than the S&P 500, as shown in the stock return chart in Figure 2.1.

As Danaher describes in its 2013 10K filing:

> We use a set of lean, leadership, and growth tools and processes, known as the DANAHER BUSINESS SYSTEM ("DBS"), which are designed to continuously improve business performance in the critical areas of quality, delivery, cost and innovation. Within the DBS framework, we pursue a number of ongoing strategic initiatives relating to idea generation, product development and commercialization, global sourcing of materials and services, manufacturing improvement and sales and marketing.[†]

So what about others? Since the 1980s many other companies outside of Japan have tried to adopt TPS, or Lean, as we call it today, with mixed

---

[*] Reuters Investment Profile Report, Danaher, March 21, 2014.
[†] Danaher 2013 Annual Report, 10K Filing, p. 3.

> ### Lean Acronym Box
>
> PDCA—Plan, Do Check, Act
> SMED—Single Minute Change of Dies
> DMAIC—Define, Measure, Analyze, Improve, Control
> TPM—Total Productive Maintenance
> VSM—Value Stream Mapping

results. *Industry Week* surveys have found 75% of manufacturers are doing some continuous improvement programs. Many have started using some of the 70 or more Lean or Six Sigma tools and training their workforce in 5S, the 5 whys, PDCA, single-minute exchange of dies (SMED), DMAIC, TPM, value stream mapping (VSM), Poka-Yoke, standard work, Kanban, and more. Some spent fortunes on Lean training providers, implemented consultants, rearranged factories, and hailed the improvement results. Unfortunately, however, when the leader driving the effort moves on over time, without the passion in the company to sustain it, performance begins to decline.

According to an AlixPartners senior executives survey[*] conducted in June 2011 on the effectiveness of manufacturing improvement programs, nearly 70% of manufacturing executives reported their manufacturing improvement efforts led to a reduction in manufacturing costs of 4% or less—below what AlixPartners states is the typical minimum threshold for successful productivity programs.

The report states that more than half (53%) of respondents cited an average targeted savings of 4% or less per year (as a percentage of total manufacturing costs), or did not have defined targets. To make matters worse, it adds, 59% indicated that they anticipate less than half of expected savings to be realized and sustained. In fact, only one quarter of respondents realized a return on investment within a year or less, with over 40% unsure of the benefit brought by their program. Still, despite these poor or unknown returns on investment, more than 90% of executives surveyed considered their programs to be somewhat or very effective, indicating a substantial perception gap in this area.[*] This seems like a dangerous lack of vision and a key contributor to individual leader dependency.

---

[*] AlixPartners Publications, Senior Executive Survey: Manufacturing-Improvement Programs Effective? October 2011.

CEO Transition and Change

Take, for example, Company X, a real company that had been on the Lean journey from the beginning of 2000 up until the transition of the CEO and COO in 2011. (The company name has been changed to Company X, but financial information and data are taken from the actual annual reports and 10K filings.) The company operations were highly sought-after benchmarking tours and it had been well recognized as a Lean leader by AME, *Industry Week*, Shingo, Best Places to Work, and others over the years. It began as a privately held company, went public, and later, in 2007, again became a privately held company. The company had defined its improvement and operations management system as Company Way (CWay). The word *Lean* was included, but rarely used; it was always the CWay. The culture had developed over the years where people were energized, involved, and motivated to drive out non-value-added activities.

In 2007, the company consummated its merger with another, similar-sized company. As a result of the merger, the company's common stock ceased trading on the NYSE at the close of the market. The company merger created a larger, more diversified medical sector-focused company organized into four market segments: core product group, electronics group, implant group, and international. The resulting company revenues were doubled to almost $1 billion. The company was a leading player in its core market with a strong position in its core product group segment, and in other segments it competes with large, diversified corporations and companies that are part of corporate groups having significantly greater financial, marketing, and other resources than it does, as well as numerous smaller niche companies.

With the merger completed, the company positioned itself as capable of effectively competing in its market segments with a comprehensive range of products and the use of multiple distribution channels to grow across the four identified market segments. The company's major challenges were to deliver significant cost synergies from the merger and accelerate growth during the Great Recession, beginning in 2008–2009. The results during that period are shown in Figure 2.2, showing some growth since the recession in dollars, but a decline in EBITDA (earnings before interest, taxes, depreciation, and amortization) percentage.

The strategies were to broaden the product offering, improve market penetration for growth, and apply the principles of Lean operations to manufacturing, operating, and administrative functions to increase speed and

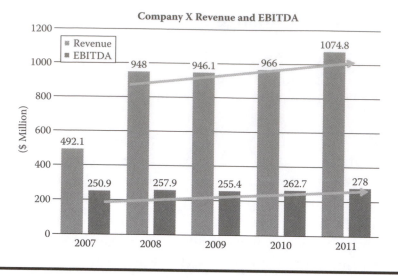

Figure 2.2　Company X revenue and EBITDA.

efficiency and reduce waste to compete in an increasingly price-sensitive healthcare industry.

During the 2007 thru 2011 period, additional product lines and companies were integrated into the company, and the CWay was the toolbox used to capture the synergies. The culture was characterized by high energy and people engaged in driving out non-value-adding activities.

Nothing stays the same, however, and in mid-year 2011 the CEO retired and the board elected to appoint a new CEO from outside the company. The COO resigned at year end the same year and was replaced by an outside VP of operations. The new CEO's challenge was somewhat of a continuation of the previous CEO, with an emphasis on growing the top line, and accelerating growth and profitability to make the company attractive to return to the public market. Through first quarter 2014 during the new CEO tenure, the company experienced modest organic top-line growth of 5.1 and 4.1% in 2012 and 2013, respectively, shown in Figure 2.3, and declining EBITDA, as shown in Figure 2.4.

The company also abandoned the Lean strategy represented in the CWay during the same 2-year period and allowed current assets (Figure 2.5) to increase by $89.5 million (26% increase), including $60.5 million in inventories. In other words, the company invested almost $90 million and earned a negative $13.8 million EBITDA return. The focus and direction of the company is to drive sales and measures that are now all financial. The CWay has been purged from the company, as have the leaders that drove the Lean

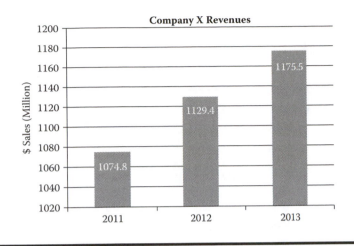

Figure 2.3 Company X revenues.

improvements in the company. The plants have shifted from operational metrics to financial metrics, emphasizing contribution margin.

In 2014, despite the previous 2 years' results, analysts are continuing to expect growth to come from new products and operating margins to benefit from the realization of merger-related synergies and other cost-saving initiatives. Some of those cost savings initiatives have been to release a number of the middle managers in operations who had been leaders in the CWay culture that the company developed over the years.

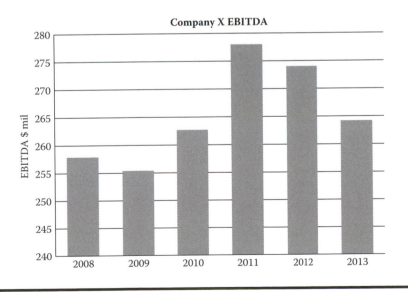

Figure 2.4 Company X EBITDA.

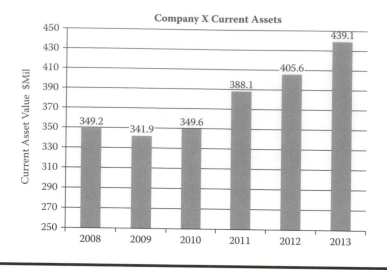

Figure 2.5 Company X current assets.

Company X launched its Lean transformation in 2000 focusing on manufacturing and distribution. With the success the operations leadership recognized that the CWay could improve all operations including product development. It played a key role in its initial public stock offering and the ability of the company to integrate numerous acquisitions. By 2011, Lean remained limited to operations and was ignored or resisted by the sales and marketing functions. Lean was not viewed as a way to counter the increased presence and pressure from global competition or a means for long-term competitive advantage. Consequently, Company X revenue growth without acquisition continued to be a challenge leading the new management to create a new plan.

The following is our discussion with the previous COO:

Status of Lean prior to CEO change:
Lean was defined in the Company Way (CWay). The goals of the CWay were to:

1. Improve customer experience
2. Improve quality
3. Reduce lead time
4. Reduce total costs

The CWay was the set of principles and behaviors that under-
lie the company's managerial approach and operations system.
The CWay began with line of sight, which begins with vision,
mission, and core values. These are connected throughout the
business, and the tools in the CWay were there to support the
line of sight. People need to know the tools in order to know
how to select the right tools to apply. The CWay was how the
company operated in operations functions, not necessarily
how sales and marketing operated. After a journey of about 11
years, it was just beginning in the sales and marketing functions. This was driven by the COO.

Why an outside CEO?

The company did not have a CEO succession plan. The owners wanted the new CEO to have experience running a $1
billion business and who had taken a company public. The
owners wanted to establish growth as part of the "go public"
story.

What has the new CEO brought to the company?

The new CEO brought a different perspective of how to make
an excellent business. His emphasis is on growth. His interest
is not in operations excellence. The new CEO's observation
when he joined the company was, "You have the All Stars in
operations. What's needed is for the All Stars to be in sales
and marketing." His emphasis is financial performance and hit-
ting the numbers and does not interact with people.

Why fire the operations middle managers?

Today the company leaders have lost the line of sight, so little
is being done to continuously improve. The company leadership direction is to go after the gopher. They stopped expecting and supporting the continuous improvement activities that
produced the funnel of cost savings and lead time improvements, and turned it into a quarterly push for the numbers
philosophy. When the company loses Lean leadership, the
organization cannot stay the course on the Lean journey.

Management teams are fragile. Even the best of teams require attention
when a new member has been brought into the organization. It changes
the team. The company has changed significantly and lost its mojo.
However, there are few businesses that do not seek to grow their revenues

(improve sales) and increase their bottom line (improve profits). At their core, the principles of focusing on customer and eliminating waste, which is the fundamental basis of Lean, apply to any work activity, as does engaging the people that actually accomplish the work. This leads us to the conclusion that whatever you call it, Lean or the Company Way, it is a management system, and continuous improvement needs to be a strong part of that system.

Focus on the Business Model

The simple principles of engaging people to focus on the customer and take waste out of the business go right to the heart of the improvement culture we would like to see in all our businesses. Yet, there remains pervasive misunderstanding that simply focusing on Lean, Six Sigma, Lean Sigma, or some other brand of continuous improvement processes alone will be the magic fix. As we see from numerous assessment tools, most continuous improvement initiatives focus too much on implementing particular checklist of tools and processes, rather than on basic execution of the business model. It is no wonder that many traditional Lean and Six Sigma programs tend to fail to institutionalize the improvements that they do generate and are lost in transitions of leadership. So if we want Lean to survive in the long term, we must look at it as a management system and not a program or a bunch of tools. Larry Fast, in his Industry Week article of July 22, 2014, states that only 2 to 3% of Lean transformations last 10 years. We would restate that to say only 2 to 3% of companies and their leadership get to the strategic point of understanding Lean as a management system. Consequently, Lean never quite delivers the desired corporate results.

So What Is a Lean Management System?

The late Peter Drucker devoted his professional life to the study of management, and he tells us, "The essence of management is not techniques and procedures. The essence of management is to make knowledge productive."* In the same text, he goes on to say that management is the distinctive organ of all organizations, and its purpose is to make human strengths productive and human weaknesses irrelevant.

The framework of policy and processes that ensures an organization can achieve its objectives is a management system. Whether we call it a traditional system or Lean system doesn't seem to matter under Drucker's definition. However, a Lean management system is one that maintains a consistent focus on creating value as well as on the processes the company uses to create and deliver that value. While most management systems focus on results, the Lean management system's additional focus on process provides the means for improving results.

A Lean management system consists of the five key elements in Figure 2.6: clarity of purpose, standard work, transparency, accountability, and innovation.

1. Clarity of purpose. The purpose of a business is to create a customer, so it is the customer who determines what the business should be. The first principle of Lean, we have learned, is that it starts with the customer, and the value of what the organization does is defined by the customer. In Lean, management strives for a collective vision of the kind of organization it seeks to be and a set of shared goals everyone strives to achieve. Strategies that support the vision and mission are developed with a line-of-sight approach, as illustrated in Figure 2.7.

   The task is to link the financial variables and result drivers into an achievement framework that is kept highly visible to everyone in the company. A strategy clearly defined and kept alive by management allows everyone to measure execution throughout each value stream, and to contribute to improving it.

   Every person in every department and work team must clearly see and understand how what they are working on today correlates to and supports the overall strategic vision. Management's role is to help everyone in the organization to see their job in the mission and strategy, so that they truly understand and are motivated by how their team's to-do list fits with their company's overarching strategic objectives. As

---

* Peter F. Drucker, *Managing in a Time of Great Change*, Truman Talley Bock Dutton, New York, 1995, p. 250.

© KDR Associates, Inc.

Core Management Model

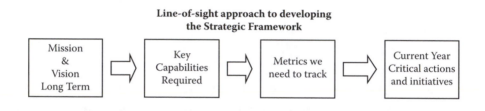

Clarity of Purpose
Why we are here? Where are we going?

Standard Work
How do we do things around here?

Transparency
What is happening?

Accountability
Can I do what I need to do?

Innovation
Product • Process • Quality of Life

Figure 2.6   Core management model.

**Line-of-sight approach to developing
the Strategic Framework**

| Mission & Vision Long Term | Key Capabilities Required | Metrics we need to track | Current Year Critical actions and initiatives |

Figure 2.7   Line-of-sight approach to developing the Strategic Framework.

an excellent example of keeping its purpose clear, Johnson & Johnson developed a credo in the 1940s that is still emphasized today in its strategic framework:

Nothing is more important than the health and well-being of those we love. That's why the Johnson & Johnson Family of Companies for more than 125 years has committed itself to caring for people. This commitment—a legacy of our founders and a very real motivating force among our employees—is embodied in Our Credo, which speaks to "our first responsibility" to the doctors, nurses, patients, the mothers and fathers and all who use our products.

The success of our enterprise is built on Our Credo and a unique set of strategic principles. We are broadly based in health care. Our focus is on managing for the long term. We operate under a decentralized management approach. And we do all this through a unique culture that values and fosters the development of our people.*

2. Standard work. A Lean management system is about developing all people to see and solve problems. Taiichi Ohno, Toyota engineer who later became president of Toyota Motor Corporation, in his book related how he began by getting workers to carefully observe work and write their own standard, and then be able to coach others to do the work. The standard was to be followed until a better method was found and became the new standard. The driver for improved standard work is problem visibility. All Lean techniques we see and hear about are intended to stimulate everyone to see a problem so that they can solve problems improving standard work at all times.

   We typically think of standard work applying only to shop floor members, but Lean is a social system that relies on the direct work process engagement of every level of the organization. In a Lean management system, standard work applies and defines the role of every team member in the operation, including leaders, which is mutually supportive, as illustrated in Figure 2.8.

   At the management level, leaders' standard work provides consistency of management practices that focus on the business processes and developing people. The investment in developing people is done by training, rotating people through roles and responsibilities that build their skills, and day-to-day coaching. Leaders' standard work establishes clear expectations and behavior that demonstrates what it means for leaders to focus on people and process. For example, daily checklists can be used by leaders at every level to reinforce coaching opportunities and to provide explicit expectations for continuously improving work processes.

   Finally, management standard work must include asking which customers' needs are not adequately satisfied by the products and services offered today—not only aiming at modifying, extending, and developing the existing ongoing business, but asking what opportunities are opening up for the business. The ability to ask these questions as a matter of practice is what makes a growth company.

---

* Johnson & Johnson Corporation, http://www.jnj.com/about-jnj/management-approach.

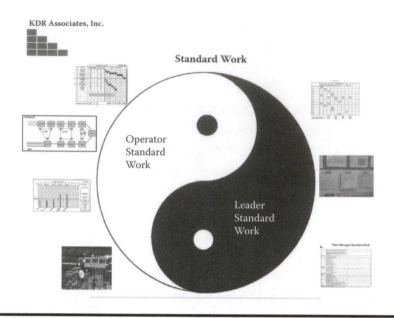

Figure 2.8   Standard work.

3. Transparency. A transparent organization is one that encourages open access to information, participation, and decision making. Such organizations exhibit the traits of honesty, respect, and admitting when they're wrong. Information is made available for people to understand what is going on at the time that they need it to do their jobs effectively. Information is made available consistently in both content and process. Surprises are avoided.

In a Lean system, visual management is the expression of transparency. Information and controls are designed to be visible to allow people to manage their own work processes. This would include making standards visible to everyone so action, and corrective action when necessary, can be taken in real time. Visual management encompasses a range of tools, such as process charts, indicators, and visual instructions that provide status, trends, and triggers for action.

One outstanding example is from two-time Baldrige National Quality Award Winner Texas Nameplate, a high-tech company in Dallas that provides nameplates for all types of product manufacturers. Its president and CEO, Dale Crownover, saw an opportunity to both address transparency and generate triggers for action. With its focus on quality and customer value, the small company of less than 100 people has a very flat organization with live production status monitors mounted overhead in all departments. As the daily drumbeat of production progresses, the

TV monitors report results, backlogs, and highlights the value stream staffing needs. The highly motivated and cross-trained staff can then move to work cells in need of help. They are guided by line of sight to the customers' orders. This best practice is beyond self-directed work teams (SDWTs); it's more like customer-focused and engaged teams and work groups.

We experience visual controls each time we pull our cars out of the garage. Streets are marked with lines and directional signs. Intersections are indicated by lights and signs. Additionally, many highways today have real-time status signage informing drivers of traffic conditions.

Consider for a moment how life on the highway would be if those controls were managed by traffic managers—instead of lights, signs, and painted lines, traffic managers were used to direct drivers' actions. It doesn't take much imagination to realize that traffic would be at a standstill, and the cost of the huge labor force to accomplish this would bankrupt most communities. Yet in our companies, visual controls are few and inconsistent at best.

Many companies focus on the end-of-month or end-of-quarter ritual where there is a great deal of data gathering, analysis, and deliberation over what happened over the past period and what will be done during the coming period. By the time the analysis and decision making is completed, much of the current period has passed. This has sometimes been characterized as "closing the gate after the horse has left the stable."

In a Lean organization, the business is focused on managing processes in real time at the place of work—the Gemba. The areas of emphasis with visual controls have a direct connection with company strategy, and are integrated into management standard work. Important business process information is recorded and displayed in simple visual terms throughout the company for all to see and react to as it happens. Typically this information includes process metrics, work instructions, and general site and company information.

Visual management is the sensing mechanism. It provides transparency of operational reality and clarity of deviations against standards of performance. Information is delivered to inform, alert, or motivate office and production teams. Most have heard the cliché "What gets measured gets managed." In a Lean environment, what gets measured visually gets managed in real time.

4. Accountability. Leaders often say that their organization's greatest asset is its people—but in reality, this is only true when those employees are fully engaged in their jobs. Gallup's* analysis in its the "State of the American Workplace 2013" report found only 30% of the workforce is engaged and feels a connection to their company. Further, it found that engaged employees having a sense of accountability to the organization, themselves, and their fellow workers drive innovation and move the organization forward.

The Lean management system is a disciplined, structured approach that provides the framework to quickly recognize opportunities and problems. The emphasis is on developing clear roles that remove ambiguity, speeds decision making, and supports engagement. People understand what is expected of them, the decisions that are theirs to make, and who they need to collaborate with to carry out their work processes to achieve desired results. The process of clarifying roles that focus on accountabilities and decision making, and then following up to close gaps rather than reviewing performance, action assignments, and static goals, is real accountability.

Lean organization structures allow organizations to focus on meaningful work and eliminate activities that do not add value. Lean structures are flatter and spans of control are wider. In a Lean culture everyone in the organization is personally committed to achieving the results the organization has targeted. With fewer organizational layers, communication and decision making are faster. People assume accountability by agreeing on the standards to which the organization members want to hold themselves and each other accountable. These include shared values, the work environment, quality, meetings, projects, and other elements important to the organization. Leaders at all levels are visible, involved, and have a better view of day-to-day operations and customer interactions. With a wider span of control, managers have no time to micromanage, but can lead, coach, and inspire people to improve the processes that define the management system.

In Lean management, real-time daily accountability goes beyond just checking to see if the target was met. It includes creating mechanisms to expose problems, eliminate them, and then repeating the

---

* Gallup, State of the American Workplace 2013, Employee Engagement Insights for U.S. Business Leaders.

cycle over and over. The activity in this environment includes brief daily, weekly, and monthly structured meetings and improvement work sessions at the team, supervisor, and management levels that keep focus on and support bottom-up participation in improvement, work plans, and accountability for performance. The meetings are structured to support what is needed by everyone involved, not just the manager.

Most work team meetings, for example, are short 5- to 15-minute stand-up sessions held in the work areas. The agendas cover sharing current status, attendance, manpower allocation, material, equipment, safety issues, and ending with the plan for the day. At the meetings, assessment is made based on data, corrective action is assigned, and accountability is reinforced.

5. Continuous improvement and innovation. The discipline to drive continuous improvement, take out waste, solve problems, and create an involved and engaged work organization is necessary to build organizational capability to deliver value. But expectations and needs of customers are constantly evolving. Management needs to constantly ask what the business should be and what opportunities are opening up or created to fulfill the purpose and mission of the business. The winners in today's market will be those that are constantly innovating both their product and service offerings and their business models around their customers.

Lean management systems are especially tuned to the voice and the experience of their customers with their businesses, products, and services. While much of work is tactical execution of the organization's strategy, the strategy is constantly challenged and adjusted as a greater understanding of the value the customer seeks is achieved. Consider where Apple would be today if it had stopped with the Mac.

A Lean management system creates a work environment for improving both work processes and learning processes to develop maximum value creation. This would include the ability to deal with new and unexpected challenges or opportunities when they occur, as well as leadership transitions. In the current volatile economic climate, the survivors will be the ones who are better at this than the others in their industry.

In summary, improvement must be driven at all levels of the organization: strategically, organizationally, and individually.

As most of us know by now, Lean is a proven way to improve operations. Yet, while users continue to tout the solid benefits and results from their Lean initiatives, many companies continue to struggle to achieve the large-scale performance change they had been seeking. The reasons are understandable. Viewed as an operations program and a set of tools, Lean efforts, while powerful, are confined to do differently what is already being done. They simply become how-to-do tools. Yet what-to-do is increasingly the central challenge facing management today. With a programmatic theme, Lean efforts in most cases typically focus on solving smaller problems rather than the bigger, more strategic issues that can generate breakthrough performance. Unless the management systems our companies employ view Lean as a strategic competitive weapon, as Toyota and Danaher have, Lean will continue to be viewed as a fad promoted by consultants and a collection of tools vulnerable to the whims of leadership changes.

Your Company?

1. Strategy: _____

2. Customers: _____

3. Leaders: _____

4. Associate engagement: _____

5. Improvement: _____

Chapter 3

Top 10 Contributors to Failure

Failure is a pretty strong word, but considering all the effort that has been invested in a Lean transformation for a few years, it is not too strong. We define a Lean failure as a management decision to limit the company's Lean efforts to certain departments and just do Lean stuff. This usually manifests itself when the company reaches the point where it must make a decision to adopt a strategy shift to Lean or give up on the Lean journey. Consider the fact that a Lean strategy is a long-term culture and commitment of company resources to achieve business success. Typically, there has been significant Lean training to orient all employees and to build their expectations from management. Not only have Lean tools been absorbed and some Lean systems have been developed into standard work, but the culture has been gradually turned to begin alignment with the two key building blocks of Lean: continuous improvement and respect for people, including management mentoring. So a failure of Lean is a significant backward step and results in the questioning of management direction. All the "I told you so" foot draggers and resistors to change now have evidence that if they wait it out, management is not really committed to long-term strategies.

We have done research on many of the companies that started down the path on a Lean transformation and failed, and we found that company leaders failed to make the strategic leap due to various factors. This chapter will list the top 10 reasons for failure, the major causes, and some techniques to mitigate them. In Table 3.1 is a quick summary that will be discussed in detail later.

Table 3.1 Top 10 Failure Modes

Failure Cause	Symptoms	Solution Techniques
1. We have arrived, arrogance	Complacency, no management passion or strategic leadership	Training, a burning platform, leadership vision, stretch goals
2. Upper management not involved	No visibility of management, no Gemba walks, no mentoring	Training by sensei, less Lean speak, benchmarking successful companies
3. Too much Lean lingo	Many people turned off and not participating	Better use of familiar business terminology, get people involved in Kaizens, sharing ideas and solving business problems, communication
4. New CEO with another plan	New CEO does not support the Lean culture	Understand the goals of the new CEO, align business model and Lean strategy to help him or her
5. Lack of recognition	People are not involved and not passionate about continuous improvement	Management needs to mentor, Gemba walk, and show appreciation for efforts; do not punish failure—in fact, support fast failure cycles of learning
6. Overuse of one tool	Referring to one specific tool in projects and meetings to the exclusion of others	Make sure Lean training clearly explains where tools should be used and not used
7. Doing Lean because everyone else does it	Lack of management passion, training, and involvement; merely checking the box; casual Lean transformation	Align Lean goals with business goals, benchmarking successful companies, outside evaluation, measures, metrics

(Continued)

Table 3.1 *(Continued)*   **Top 10 Failure Modes**

Failure Cause	Symptoms	Solution Techniques
8. Short-term cost-cutting focus	Lack of people involvement, training, and long-term business processes; low investment in resources	Accept short-term business needs and stress long-term alignment and benefits, middle management buy-in
9. Program of the month	Viewed as temporary until the next leader; management does not commit to personal change; continual reinforcement to employees is weak	The company business system needs to embrace Lean as the key approach to company management; communication and top management actions demonstrate validity
10. Lean not integrated with all business systems	Lean considered a program, not a strategy	Design your company's Lean management system (LMS) based on customer value creation and Lean strategies

Top 10 Failure Modes Discussion

1. We've arrived, been there, done that! Management is happy with the short-term results and does not expect more. This can be a very easy trap for management to fall into. With some recognition and awards, you tend to think you are the benchmark. This is the arrogance factor that can be so devastating. Along with the excitement of learning how to use the Lean tools and generating cost savings from low-hanging fruit, it is easy to think, "We have reached our goal!" The good news is that the low-hanging fruit is a good, quick payback for the investment, and the board sees it as a real benefit to the bottom line.

   The reality is that the long-term health of the company requires continuing energy. This requires management to continually challenge its business model, set new goals, recognize people, and demonstrate that Lean is a management system for the long term. Management must continue to focus on day-to-day value creation for the customer and developing employees. There is a tendency for management to drift into the comfortable position of "We've done Lean, now what else is new?" Management may ask if there is a new management philosophy that they need to be attempting, or is there a new book that they need to follow? (Yes, this book will help!) The successful companies, like Toyota, retain an understated modesty about their accomplishments and know there is a strong basic foundation that a Lean journey builds to mold the whole organization toward achieving long-term excellence. If Lean is focused only on cost cutting, it may not be deployed in all the support groups, like marketing, engineering, and quality, so there is much more to do!

2. Upper management not involved. In this failure mode, Lean training is done at all lower levels, but not with upper management involvement. If upper management does not understand their responsibilities in a Lean transformation and long-term health, they are doomed to fail. They will not understand the strategy for strengthening the business, the use of the tools, the benefits to expect, and the time involved in problem solving and learning and understanding the vocabulary. They will feel Lean is simply one of the how-to-do approaches their people are using and not get involved.

   Worse yet, upper management will not take personal responsibility to look for waste and model their behavior for all those close to them to follow. Senior management is more directive and expects everyone else to make Lean happen. They set goals, but do not clear barriers. They are managing and not leading. Here again, the early successes and resulting savings may convince them that they are successful and have done the right things, so they put their attention on other things. However, the real performance breakthroughs come as the obvious quick fixes disappear. So what the organization needs is true leadership to mentor and help it to see waste in all processes. A question to ask here is: "Has management changed their own behaviors to manage in a Lean way?"

3. Too much Lean lingo. As people are trained in Lean concepts there are many terms, tools, and concepts that are unique and strange to a person not as well trained. Management's language is centered on the business terms we covered in Chapter 1, and their decisions will be based on the business terms. Too much Lean lingo can develop into a cult-type atmosphere and seem like insiders vs. outsiders. Those on the outside may tend to resist and actually undermine the efforts of those they see as insiders. The Lean lingo may sound strange and can lose its true meaning if overused by folks that may not fully understand. It

can cause a cultural split among management people and also among employees. Comprehensive training is needed to help get everyone on board with the direction of the organization and why. Upper management behavior will be watched closely to see if they "walk the talk." One company senior manager, for example, had an aversion to the Japanese terms. At the time Just-in-Time was the hot rage. So the Lean practitioner used continuous flow instead of Just-in-Time, and the manager adopted it on his program.

In the Lean transformation environment, Lean must be adapted to the current culture so that it fits in and becomes the way people work—so we are not throwing away everything that has been keeping the business operating. Cultures will tend to act like the human body in a medical sense. Antibodies will be called in to attack what the body sees as a foreign disease invasion or, in our case, change. Adapting the organization and individuals to change is very important. Learning and changing behavior by including people in making change happen, especially involvement in changing their own work processes and recognition of contributions, will help fight off the antibodies! As we discuss later, it is important for the Lean practitioner to be able to speak the language of management and understand the business so that projects can focus on true large business problems. Everyone in the continuous improvement process needs to speak in business terms and use the proper Lean tools to overcome barriers.

4. New CEO with another plan. One of the most destructive approaches we've seen by a new CEO, president, or operations manager is for him or her to arrive on the scene and declare, "We don't do Lean anymore." He or she may have been involved in a Lean failure elsewhere or may have been an outsider or may have heard of a failure from a friend. The Malcolm Baldrige National Quality Award started in 1990, and after a few years of great success and national recognition, a former Baldrige winner went into financial trouble. All the naysayers came out of the woodwork and declared, "See the Baldrige is not good," when in fact, the company was still executing well in all its internal processes, but its market had deteriorated and it was not responsive enough to adapt. The original Baldrige award criterion was focused on internal quality, not on the overall company business model and its ability to be responsive to changing markets. The same thing can happen with a Lean transformation; naysayers will quickly point to the negatives to discount the value of Lean. One of these may be the new CEO.

The first question to ask of a new leader is: "What are your goals and priorities?" Surely the new guy wants the organization to be productive and profitable and work aggressively on customer needs. Several companies deep into the Lean transformation have been redirected by a new leader and with widely varying results. The biggest casualty is the culture that has been carefully groomed to look for waste in an organized fashion, problem-solve effectively, look for value stream flow, and aggressively work with customers to meet their needs. So the next question to ask is, are these not core values of any business?

CEOs like strategy and are concerned about costs and drivers to achieve growth. Creating competitive advantage to facilitate growth is a desired result of any strategy. A Lean transformation led by management that sees Lean strategically will adopt Lean across the company's organizations for process improvements, leadership development, and growth. Surely all business processes can be improved, so the right question a new CEO should ask is: "What is the best way to improve?" Abandoning Lean can be a company disaster if the result is to stop what is working, along with trying to fix what is not.

The old cliché "Throwing the baby out with the bathwater" comes to mind here.

5. Lack of recognition. Lean is really built on respect for people, including individuals that contribute their knowledge to solving the organization's problems and taking personal responsibility, including taking risks and mentoring others. The organization must step up to recognize and reward individuals that are contributing to the goals of the organization. We all like the vision of the leader, coach, and mentor that asks questions that lead individuals to think and see opportunities much better. The Gemba walk example of top management taking the time to listen and value opinions, rather than direct solutions from on high, provides insight on one way to recognize people's contributions and value their input. If our employees have an idea and a strong commitment to see it through even though there may be many failures, this is a meaningful trait in a Lean company. Experimentation was a hallmark in the early Toyota Motor Corporation.

Most have heard the stories of how Thomas Edison conducted thousands of trials to develop the light bulb. The WD-40 Company is a great example of persistence and promoting fast failure in order to learn fast through many cycles of learning. That's the cornerstone of the leading innovative companies. The WD-40 executives describe how the product name was derived. They relate that it took 39 tries before the right formula was discovered, reminding us that they had 39 failures before success—hence their brand name! From the simply-communicate.com website* we hear the real story:

Norm Larsen, a scientist at the Rocket Chemical Company, San Diego, was attempting to concoct a formula for displacing water and preventing corrosion in the early 1950s.

It was on his fortieth attempt that he was met with success, hence the name: *Water-Displacement 40.* The spray has created ripples in the market ever since.

How many of us would have the same patience and given management support in that dramatic case? Do we recognize the attempt to improve or only the results?

6. Overuse of one tool. We've seen some Lean practitioners that tend to use the one favorite tool that they understand to the exclusion of other, more appropriate tools. For example, there was an engineer who loved Six Sigma variability charts. The problem occurred when there was some waste in processing steps, but he still would cling to variability charts rather than concentrating on elimination of the non-value-adding steps. Another person liked Pareto analysis to the exclusion of many other approaches. The old quote "If you have a hammer, everything looks like a nail" rings true, and we must be careful that our people know when tools are appropriate and when some are not.

Raytheon, in 1998, combined Lean, Six Sigma, and change management into what it called Raytheon Six Sigma™, which at the time was a good reference for Wall Street investors to associate with and resounded with what Jack Welch was doing at GE. It trained its change agents in all the tools of the three disciplines and created what is now called Lean Sigma in many quarters. Raytheon didn't want a Lean tools vs. Six Sigma tools debate that would deflect the focus from its overall goal of continuous improvement. Raytheon wanted to use the right tool at the right time in order to make the most improvement in the business processes. Having everyone using the same terminology and language across five previous companies—Raytheon, Texas Instruments Defense and Electronic Systems, E-Systems, General Dynamics–San Diego, and

---

* www.simply-communicate.com.

Hughes Aircraft—was important in order to create a new culture and management model. The benefit was that this new culture of Raytheon Six Sigma™ put all previous experts on the same footing and required everyone to learn rapidly to reestablish their credentials. Agile experts, Six Sigma Black Belts, and Lean experts all had to become Raytheon Six Sigma experts to go forward. What Raytheon found through its experience was that most process improvements could be addressed with Lean tools before trying to apply the more mathematically demanding Six Sigma tools. This sped up the improvement process tremendously. It found it could make changes faster!

7. Doing Lean because everyone else does. Before signing up for Lean, upper management needs to understand the comprehensive changes required in the way it personally does business. It is not a program that can be run by some mid-level manager and results reviewed in monthly and quarterly meetings. It's a life-changing event or series of events and is truly a journey, as we have talked about. A Lean transformation takes a lot of commitment from leaders and managers, and there needs to be a real burning platform well understood by both management and all employees.

    The burning platform needs to be explained so that continuous improvement is expected and part of the "way we work," so that everyone understands and appreciates what this will do for the company and what this will do for them personally. Any change can be approached from a motherhood and apple pie standpoint. It's for the good of all, it's for our country, it's good for the company, and so forth, but that will only go so far these days. It also must be explained on a personal benefit level, i.e., "I will be more employable in the future; I will have more skills if I do this"—especially since we've found that Generation Y folks will ask, "What's in it for me?" right up front. If your company is going into Lean, but paying lip service in order to be able to say, "Yes, we are Lean," and merely checking the box, then it will fail. Doing Lean stuff is not a strategy!

8. Short-term cost-cutting focus. If you talk to many people on the street like we have, you will frequently hear the misconception that Lean is about reducing job satisfaction, cutting jobs, and closing plants. There have been Lean implementations that were so successful at cutting costs that that became what was advertised and promoted. The casual observer and casual implementer will focus on cost cutting only. Like we discussed earlier, picking the low-hanging fruit can and will attract attention and motivate people, and that is the easy part. But the long-term culture change is more important to survival and building a robust

company to focus on growth. Using each and every employee to work toward continuous improvement and focus on providing customer value pays continuing dividends for the long term.

Lean has picked up a bad reputation in some circles because of the cost-cutting reputation and what it might mean to individuals, jobs, and quality of life. The old slogan "Lean and mean" is a bad slogan when trying to create a Lean culture. A successful Lean program will focus on long-term customer value creation utilizing continuous improvement and respect for people and everyone feeling good about themselves when they go home at night. In no way should it be mean! A Lean culture is customer-centric with an engaged workforce continually driving out waste to create capacity for growth and creating wealth. In the long run, cost cutting rarely creates growth or wealth.

9. This is just another "program of the day." At companies that have been successful in the Lean strategy for the long term, like Danaher, Autoliv, and Toyota, we see they have successfully transcended the program-of-the-day syndrome because of their continued focus and implementation of a comprehensive Lean management system (LMS), described in Chapter 2. But for companies beginning and even through the first 5 years, we still consider them in the organizational transformation to a Lean culture. Lean transformation is a major change for most.

Anytime major change occurs we've all seen early adopters, people sitting on the fence, and those actively dragging their feet. This is the historic breakdown that we have noticed during many changes introduced by management in many different organizations. This is depicted in Figure 3.1.

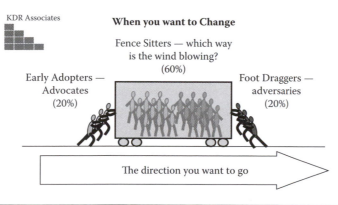

Figure 3.1   When you want to change.

a. Usually about 20% of employees are early adopters and are excited to try something new; they have passion and positive energy and can carry the ball to get everything started. It's important to energize this group on the value and vision of the Lean journey and their role.

b. About 60% are willing to participate, but are not fully committed. We call them fence sitters. They will do tasks and try not to offend anyone, but they are intently looking at which way the wind is blowing and are very observant of the actions of upper management, on a day-by-day basis. They will look to see allocation of resources, especially management's time, interest, budgets, and communications. Every management action they see will drive them either toward adoption or away from it. They keep score on a daily basis to see who is winning. After all, there have been many new programs tried before, and most failed after a year or two. Some will say silently, "I can wait this out until we get a new leader." The sad thing is that many new potentially good programs do not succeed, and this builds the community skepticism that we see.

c. About 20% are foot draggers and are working against any new program. They do not like change. They actively do not want to do anything new and will work either visibly or invisibly against their success. It's best to identify these people and isolate them from others, convert them to team players, or help them find a new job. These people will say, "This will not work!" and try to spread their ideas among other employees to gain support.

By benchmarking other companies on the Lean journey, management can come to understand that the journey is long and requires constant reinforcement. Too many companies feel like they must be perfect, but do not really understand that others are going through some of the same challenges, trials, and tribulations. They may not want to reveal shortcomings and problems to others. But by using the APQC Benchmarking Code of Conduct* they can feel protected for sharing this information publicly. By sharing best practices and lessons learned, we can get a reality check that it requires hard work, and others may have already solved the problems we are currently experiencing. By benchmarking your Lean journey in other industries, you can see that there are common problems and unique solutions that you may not have discovered yet! Raytheon was able to learn a lot about rapid product

---

* www.apqc.org.

development from Intel and manufacturing shop Lean transformation from Newport News Shipbuilding. They also learned about Six Sigma deployments from Allied Signal (now part of Honeywell) and General Electric (Michael English and William H. Baker, 2006).[*]

Successful long-term Lean companies like Toyota and Danaher have installed Lean business systems and defined their expectations in standard work and processes while listening to employees' ideas, suggestions, and improvements. Upper management is committed and involved and continues communications to reinforce their business system. Benchmarking them and reading about their journeys can help convince both upper management and mid-level managers to get on the train.

10. Lack of integrating Lean as part of the company business strategy, creating a Lean management system (LMS). We saved this failure mode until last to emphasize its long-term importance. Some of the most successful long-term success stories, such as Danaher, Toyota, and Raytheon, have created their own business systems that are based on Lean and are applicable across all functions in the business. Danaher has been on the Lean journey since the mid-1980s and has been very successful for the long term. Early on, it created the Danaher Business System (DBS) to focus on customers' priorities: quality, delivery, cost, and innovation. The DBS evolved to incorporate improvement tools and a philosophy, a set of values, and a series of management processes that define how they work across all functions of the business. These DBS tools are based on:

1. Growth
2. Leadership
3. Lean

The DBS is deployed both within the company and in all its divisions and new acquisitions, thus providing a blueprint for a smooth transition (Danaher website, 2014).

In April 2014 the current CEO, Lawrence Culp, Jr., announced his retirement in 2015, and his successor, Thomas P. Joyce, Jr., a seasoned teacher and practitioner of DBS has played a key role in creating and evolving many of the DBS tools and processes on which the system is built (Danaher press release, 2014). The DBS is deeply embedded in the

---

[*] Michael English and William H. Baker, Jr. *Winning the Knowledge Transfer Race*, McGraw-Hill, New York, 2006.

culture and management system and is frequently promoted to investors as Danaher's way of expanding capabilities to drive consistent execution and sustain outstanding results. Lean is a major building block and part of succession planning; it is hard to see how it would abandon the Lean journey. This is a clear commitment.

We have outlined the top 10 failure modes above that we have seen and been part of with the intention that the reader can recognize these patterns early, like early warning radar, and be able to take positive actions to counter any threat against Lean for the long term. A Lean culture should not be threatening to anyone, but should be seen as a strategic investment that will pay back many times over in a dynamic forward-looking, agile, customer- and employee-centered leading-edge organization.

As a reference, we looked at other views of what it takes to produce a successful Lean strategy. In *Beyond the Lean Transformation* by Deborah J. Nightingale and Jayakanth Srinivasan, we see their seven principles of a successful enterprise transformation in Chapter 3, as listed in Table 3.2 (Nightingale and Srinivasan, 2011).

Indeed, these are good keys to having a successful Lean transformation, but we would also stress they are important even if you have been on a successful 5- to 10-year journey in order to sustain it for the long term. By embedding Lean deeply and institutionalizing it into the culture, like Danaher, Lean can develop roots. We see that by creating a business system with Lean roots and beliefs, or what we call a Lean management system, there is an understanding that it is "the way we work" and it is here to stay!

In Table 3.3 we've provided a self-evaluation form that you can use to rate yourself to see if all the enablers are being used and to what extent.

Table 3.2   Seven Principles of a Successful Enterprise Transformation

Adopt a holistic approach
Secure leadership commitment to drive and institutionalize enterprise behaviors
Identify relevant stakeholders and determine their value propositions
Focus on enterprise effectiveness before efficiency
Address internal and external enterprise interdependencies
Ensure stability and flow within and across the enterprise
Emphasize organizational learning

Table 3.3 Self-Evaluation: Enablers of a High-Performance Lean Enterprise

Key Elements	Evaluation Characteristic	No Action 0	Major Weakness 1	Neutral 2	Some Strength 3	Major Strength 4	Score Characteristic	Score Element
Top management support	Strategy development and review process clearly defined	○	○	○	○	○		Combined total ÷ 4
	Alignment and line of sight of strategic goals in organization	○	○	○	○	○		
	Associates have time allocated to work on improvement projects	○	○	○	○	○		
	Management creates environment where associates can evolve	○	○	○	○	○		
Communication	High level of two-way communications throughout the organization	○	○	○	○	○		Combined total ÷ 3

(Continued)

Table 3.3 (Continued) Self-Evaluation: Enablers of a High-Performance Lean Enterprise

Key Elements	Evaluation Characteristic	No Action	Major Weakness	Neutral	Some Strength	Major Strength	Score	
		0	1	2	3	4	Characteristic	Element
	Management visible and available to associates	o	o	o	o	o		
	Company plans are well developed and understood by all associates	o	o	o	o	o		
Middle management buy-in	Behavior reinforces continuous company improvement	o	o	o	o	o		Combined total ÷ 4
	Supervisors and managers routinely train associates	o	o	o	o	o		
	Key drivers for performance are identified and tracked	o	o	o	o	o		
	Barriers to improvement are removed quickly and humanely	o	o	o	o	o		

								Combined total ÷ 3
Customer focus	Teamwork across all functions drives customer satisfaction	o	o	o	o	o	o	Combined total ÷ 3
	Mission clearly understood by all and focused on customer	o	o	o	o	o	o	
	Roadblocks to customer satisfaction are actively worked	o	o	o	o	o	o	
Culture	Associates recognized as the most valuable resource	o	o	o	o	o	o	Combined total ÷ 3
	Decision making is delegated to the lowest possible levels in the company	o	o	o	o	o	o	
	Accountability, credit, responsibility, and ownership are shared	o	o	o	o	o	o	

(Continued)

Table 3.3 (Continued) Self-Evaluation: Enablers of a High-Performance Lean Enterprise

Key Elements	Evaluation Characteristic	No Action 0	Major Weakness 1	Neutral 2	Some Strength 3	Major Strength 4	Score Characteristic	Score Element
Measures/ Metrics	Common key measures are used by all for improvement	o	o	o	o	o		Combined total ÷ 3
	Measures are tied to company goals and budget	o	o	o	o	o		
	Measures are displayed in work areas	o	o	o	o	o		
CI/Lean leadership	Managers are good examples of CI/Lean practices	o	o	o	o	o		Combined total ÷ 3
	In-house CI/Lean facilitators are developed	o	o	o	o	o		
	All associates are trained to use problem-solving tools for improvement	o	o	o	o	o		

							Combined total ÷ 3
People	Training is viewed as a critical investment	o	o	o	o	o	Combined total ÷ 3
	Performance evaluation based on desired CI/Lean behaviors	o	o	o	o	o	
	Promotions are based on contribution to company improvement	o	o	o	o	o	
Change mechanisms	Kaizen is used to accomplish improvement daily	o	o	o	o	o	Combined total ÷ 3
	Kaizen events are used in preproduct/process stage	o	o	o	o	o	
	People are coached, advised, and trained in tools to make improvements	o	o	o	o	o	
Reward and pay systems	Goal achievement is recognized and celebrated	o	o	o	o	o	Combined total ÷ 3

(Continued)

Table 3.3 (Continued) Self-Evaluation: Enablers of a High-Performance Lean Enterprise

Key Elements	Evaluation Characteristic	No Action	Major Weakness	Neutral	Some Strength	Major Strength	Score	
		0	1	2	3	4	Characteristic	Element
	Associates can and do self-performance evaluation	o	o	o	o	o		
	Bonus system is aligned with company CI/Lean goals	o	o	o	o	o		
Progress		0					Sum total	Combined

Takeaways

- Has your company embedded Lean deeply in its business system, so that it's not a program of the month?

- Is management totally committed by communicating and committing their resources and time?

- Is everyone trained on the use of proper tools, creating systems, and understanding the principles of Lean?

- Does everyone understand that Lean is a long, difficult journey that requires everyone to change?

- Are change agents/Lean practitioners recognized for taking risks as well as achieving results?

- Is knowledge shared and fast learning encouraged?

Chapter 4

Achieving Alignment

How Lean Practitioners and Business Executives Can Communicate

In this chapter we will discuss closing the gap between Lean practitioners and top management. Communication has always been the key to effective action and coordinating others' activities. Since any organization faces communication problems and barriers, what is the secret sauce to success?

> Information flow is the lifeblood of your company because it enables you to get the most out of your people and learn from your customers.[*]
>
> **—Bill Gates and Collins Hemmingway**

> It takes two people to speak the truth—one to speak and another to hear.[†]
>
> **—Henry David Thoreau**

These two quotations, one tied to the information age and one from 165 years ago, can help us understand the importance of good communication in today's fast-moving, ever-changing world.

---

[*] Bill Gates and Collins Hemmingway, *Business @ the Speed of Thought*, Warner Books, New York, 1999.

[†] Henry David Thoreau, *A Week on the Concord and Merrimack Rivers*, 1849. Reprint Viking Press, New York, 1985.

Certainly we want our Lean efforts to contribute to the lifeblood of the company while getting the most out of our people and learning from our customers, so we need to achieve excellence in our communications skills both up the company hierarchy and down. Knowledge transfer within the organization is now a key core competency and can be the competitive advantage as we operate with increasing speed and learning. Of course, knowledge transfer is based on our communication skills and utilizing all the media choices we have at our fingertips today. We've always had hand-written notes, newspapers, face-to-face meetings, and the telephone in our lifetime. Now we've added the capability to communicate by the Internet, computers, web pages, PowerPoint slides via SlideShare, mobile smart phones, iPads, e-mails, texting, and social media like Twitter, Facebook, LinkedIn, and others. So we have choices on how to communicate both up and down the company organization. We've seen managers that do not effectively work their e-mails or other new technology means, so using e-mail and new technology to communicate with them would be a los-ing choice. Generation Y folks communicate through their favorite media of texting. We must consider what media will be effective to the intended audience, and this is an important choice! In the future there will be new options to consider and use, so we must continue to adapt and change. In most cases multiple media are needed to reach the entire intended audience. Repetitive communication is also valuable to reinforce the message. Tell them what you are going to tell them, tell them, and tell them what you told them—communicate, communicate, communicate, and then communicate some more!

We found that defining common ground and common interests, and a common language to discuss those interests (see Chapter 1), is the building block that needs to be in place first before anyone can hear what someone else is speaking.

Lean Practitioner Communication Guidelines

Too often the Lean practitioners become so enthusiastic while leading contin-uous improvement (CI) projects and the learning that "Lean speak" takes over in most business discussions. There is real excitement and passion linked to identifying waste—Muri, Muda, and Mari, running Kaizens, and investigat-ing Poka-Yoke situations. But those who are not in the immediate discussion, many times, are put off by all the terminology. This can be particularly true of upper management, the CEO, and the board of directors. Lean orientation training for top executives may not make them feel comfortable to talk or listen in these "foreign" languages. Even if they have been to extensive training, they may not have absorbed the terms into their vocabulary; so they find it difficult to listen or consider it too operational or detailed. The only real way to be comfortable with Lean terms is to use them. Using the terms while on a team addressing a specific goal or becoming knowledgeable enough to teach the concepts yourself, like the Danaher executives, as explained in Chapter 3, is the best way to be comfortable with them.

The adept Lean practitioner needs to be intensely aware of this potential barrier to communication and adapt his or her communication and language to each and every management person in the discussion or witnessing a presentation. Some managers will not ask questions for fear of showing their ignorance or lack of understanding to you or their peers. Our common goal is to include and involve everyone, so a Lean practitioner needs to put into a business context what he or she is doing and how a Lean tool set is being applied in the situation he or she is working to drive results. For example, if the team is working to break a logjam of projects in product development with Lean project management tools, the Lean practitioner needs to lead the team discovery and explain without being asked.

In another example, if discussing sales lead management and turnaround time to respond to an inquiry, salespeople understand the concept of "striking while the iron is hot." It may take some explanation for them to relate to a repeatable process and the cycle time metric.

A good process for the Lean practitioner when talking about Lean projects follows:

1. Begin with the end in mind, not the journey. Before you start, scope the project in terms of how it ties to the goals of the company. How does this help the business? In your discussion, link the continuous improvement project to the policy deployment goals of the organization. If there are major strategic business metrics that are reported, which one does this project affect?
2. Understand the depth of Lean communication knowledge of the person or group and adjust to their perspective.
3. Identify the magnitude of the project or situation in terms of dollars, or customer impact, especially potential benefits or potential negatives. Most top managers look at risk vs. reward as a measuring stick for allocating resources—including Lean practitioners and time and dollars.

4. Proceed at a pace required for everyone to grasp the continuous improvement points. Ask questions to stimulate the group's interaction to attain understanding of how the Lean principles can drive results.

For a company to develop a long-term Lean organizational culture, it is imperative that all upper management be participants, models of behavior, and mentors to the other employees. In-depth training at the top levels is important, including management working on projects, reporting results, and mentoring others. That is the approach that Raytheon took, and the lower levels and mid-management became impatient to learn the new Raytheon Six Sigma™ strategy because so much time was spent bringing top management on board. They did not see the bottom-up training they had been accustomed to. This was the right approach for Raytheon so that upper management would appreciate the work involved in the Lean journey and would know what questions to ask when mentoring.

Other companies, such as Danaher, approach the top-level learning by emphasizing top management participation in rapid improvement events and requiring functional managers to become the "Lean expert" in a Lean tool as a way to develop organizational Lean competence. An example of this would be for the senior materials manager or VP to become the expert in Kanban systems. Another thing to remember is that adopting a Lean culture in a Lean management system (LMS) is an overall company strategy and not merely a set of tools and mechanics using those tools, as discussed in previous chapters.

Upper Management Communication Guidelines

So on the top management side of the communications we want upper management to be aware of and address the individual and group needs of those below them and to be able to speak in their terms. Ideally the CEO and functional heads, such as the CFO, CMO, COO, CTO, etc., develop the understanding and capability to lead improvement events and train others in the company as we have seen in Toyota. With Danaher we see the CEO and his team explaining to investors and Wall Street analysts how Danaher Business System (DBS) tools create growth and earnings in the company during their investor and analyst presentations.

The Lean practitioner, therefore, is a valuable resource to the CEO, and his senior management team can add dramatically to the achievement of the company goals. Leading Lean companies have designated fast-track executives and routed them to be Lean practitioners, so that they are steeped in Lean knowledge and experience they can use in future assignments.

David Shaner is a world-renowned teacher, Olympic skier, Fulbright Fellow, and Herring Professor of Asian Studies and Philosophy at Furman University. From his book *The Seven Arts of Change: Leading Business Transformation That Lasts* (Shaner, 2010), we learned:

> Change efforts fail when the spirit of the company remains the same.

David explains:

> Your spirit is the sum of all your beliefs, your convictions, your moral codes and your standards. All lasting transformation begins there because, ultimately, your spirit and mine is the driver of all our behavior. (Shaner, 2010)

While Shaner is referring to our individual spirit, the same applies to organizations. This is why change is so hard!

Maybe you have heard this saying:

> Culture rules policy.

Every company and organization has a culture—many times multiple cultures that vary from site to site. These cultures have been developed over many years and are so strong that they give each location its identity. We see this many times when cultural conflicts arise with company acquisitions. Like it or not, however, without concerted management effort, company cultures will develop. The culture that develops this can distinguish the company or at worst hurt it. Concerted management effort is required to guide company culture development and takes several years to change. Issuing a simple management policy does not promote change. A true culture transformation, according to Shaner, requires that your beliefs, your convictions, your moral codes, and your standards change. Our interpretation of how these tie together and definitions follow.

Organizations are made up of people with different backgrounds and lifelong experiences. And, organizations are always changing as people leave and new people join, including senior management. As a result, the organization culture is in constant change. Customers and their expectations are also continually changing as well. In a Lean transformation, top management must be aware of how their actions support or undermine the desired company core values and practices. Employees, including Lean practitioners, view and evaluate senior management actions and decisions as an indication of their intentions and long-term resolve and commitment to a Lean strategy. This is why Lean or any organizational change effort is not an overnight effort. Lean transformation is, in fact, a constant effort, as we have seen in Toyota for almost 70 years and Danaher for going on 30 years.

Common Ground

So what do we have at this point of the discussion? We may have Lean practitioners who are excited about the tools of the Lean trade—Kaizens, value stream mapping, A-3s, Poka-Yoke techniques, one-piece flow, eliminating waste, single-minute exchange of dies (SMED), and voice of the customer (VOC)—and the dollar savings that they have generated. They think this is great. They think they are doing exactly what management has asked them to do.

But do they understand the link to the business goals? Are they focusing on making improvements to current business processes or products? Are they developing people for the future and linking their efforts to critical business goals? These are critical!

And do Lean practitioners understand the basic pillars of a Lean culture that all the tools are supposed to support? Here are the top two:

- Respect for people
- Continuous improvement every day

Respect for people is often overlooked and not understood well by Lean practitioners. Most of the Lean training courses do not emphasize this important aspect or include it in workshops. By building trust and mutual respect, we can develop people to the maximum of their capabilities, and they can actively participate in bringing new ideas to the team. Toyota was very willing to host benchmarking visits and share its tools because it felt that people could see the use of the myriad tools, but no one could easily replicate the culture and the fabric of molding the CI tools and the cultural respect for people successfully. Lean leaders should have this as one of their key goals, regardless of the immediate cost savings in the heat of the battle.

The old saying is that you have to survive the quarter to allow time to make your long-term goals. While this may seem trite, it remains true that management and boards of public and some privately held companies are constantly held accountable for their business results. Those results are achieved by the accumulated contributions of the people in the organization. Unfortunately, as we have seen in the Gallup survey referenced in Chapter 2, people are the most undervalued asset in many companies. Companies routinely underestimate the capabilities of the people that work for them in spite of the fact that frequently we've seen production team members that are school board members, church leaders, and city councilmen in their personal life that have not been asked to contribute prior to Lean and teaming transformations. High-performance organizations and companies create a culture of inclusion and respect by utilizing the strengths and abilities of the entire workforce in order to achieve their goals. An older term is an *empowered workforce*! Lean practitioners need to emphasize respect for people in their daily management and continuous improvement projects and change efforts. Leaders should make it a management practice of sharing information, rewards, and power with team members so the members can take initiative, make decisions to solve problems, and improve service and performance. This goes beyond soliciting input from the team members doing the work, listening to their ideas, and involving them in the solutions. Basically high performance organizations create the expectation that its members contribute to improving the organization performance. That is real respect. Gary Convis, former managing officer of Toyota and president of Toyota Motor Manufacturing Kentucky, said, "I believe that management has no more critical role than to motivate and engage large numbers of people to work together toward a common goal."[*][†] The Lean practitioner needs to consider himself or herself as part of management in this instance, for they are implementing top management's Lean transformation strategy!

The continuous improvement pillar of Lean invokes all the tools we have been talking about, but its core principle is to challenge everything in an environment of continuous learning that embraces change! What we want to do is get away from silo and marginal thinking. Marginal thinking is the mistake "dinosaur" businesses have made that Clayton Christensen points out in his disruptive business theory:

---

[*] Jeffrey Liker, *The Toyota Way*, McGraw-Hill, New York, 2004, preface.
[†] Jeffrey Liker and Gary L. Convis, *The Toyota Way to Lean Leadership: Achieving and Sustaining Excellence Through Leadership Development*, McGraw-Hill, New York, 2012.

No company deliberately sets out to let itself be overtaken by its competitors. Rather, they are seemingly innocuous decisions that were made years before that led them down that path.

And at the end of the day, a Lean management system creates a work environment for improving both work processes and learning processes to develop maximum value creation. This would include the ability to deal with new and unexpected challenges and opportunities when they occur, as well as leadership transitions. In the current volatile economic climate, the survivors will be the ones who are better at this than the others in their industry.

This is the culture that leads to a sustainable organization that is continually adapting to a changing business environment. It is also very fragile and can be derailed and misdirected easily, which must be understood by both Lean practitioners and management alike.

A few years ago Peter Senge published his book on the learning organization, *The Fifth Discipline* (Senge, 1990). He became renowned for his breakthrough concepts and has had a major impact on corporate thinking. His interview with Bill O'Brien, then CEO of Hanover Insurance, yielded this enlightening response:

> If you believe as we did that there is an enormous reservoir of untapped potential in people that can be channeled more productively, you try to build a value-based, vision-driven environment.

Senge built what he called a discipline to explain the building blocks of achieving a shared vision. This visual model helps explain what it takes to achieve the shared vision that we are striving for in a Lean organization. In Figure 4.1 there are three levels starting at the base of the pyramid, as shown.

Figure 4.1 Building a shared vision of the future. (Peter Senge, *The Fifth Discipline: The Art and Practice of the Learning Organization*, Currency Doubleday, New York, 1990.

Table 4.1 Peter Senge's Shared Vision Detail Steps

Practices Level—Base
Acknowledging current reality and the burning platform
Individual's visioning process
Principles Level—Mid
Gain commitment vs. compliance
Create a shared vision
Essences Level—Peak
Create an employee partnership
Define a commonality of purpose (actions to achieve the shared vision)

Looking in detail at the pyramid in Table 4.1, we see that by starting at the practices level by acknowledging the current reality, the organization has a baseline point. This is important because everyone may not be at the same reality. Most often they are not! One department may be doing great, and one may not see outside customers at all. It is management's job to clarify and educate people in the current business reality, so everyone can understand the situation and buy-in. The education and sharing process allows everyone to help create their own vision of the future.

Close attention to practices that demonstrate the way work gets done and how customers are treated and people listened to are vital. We see culture change to be a continuous process and driven by focusing on behavior. In a Lean organization culture, continually emphasizing customer value and the processes used to deliver that value are how results are achieved. This approach builds a strong corporate culture.

In Senge's principles level, after people experience the practices level and through much discussion and facilitation, a shared vision can be developed. Then people can feel part of the vision and can become committed to making it happen rather than just following orders by complying.

Thus, when the organization reaches Senge's essence level—at the top of the pyramid—management forms a partnership with all the employees and the organization is committed to a common purpose and a pathway to get there is clear. This profound philosophy is simple in form, but it requires continual management effort and awareness to build Senge's learning organization with this shared vision.

Figure 4.2   The burning platform awakening.

An outcome of Senge's research is that many company leaders have recognized the vital importance of a learning organization. Senge's research is driving much of the organizational theory of today and is at the heart of the Lean pillars—respect for people and continuous improvement. The "learning organization" may be considered a buzzword, but it is considered a key management goal in many companies.

After the initial phases in a Lean transformation, the top management team may see all the Lean practitioner activity and may be excited about the initial improvements and cost savings that have been turned into dollars. They may also fear the easy savings are diminishing. This time frame can vary and may take a few years. The reality may be that management has had it easy and did not have to spend much time mentoring and cultivating the belief changes we talked about earlier.

Let's look at what management should be doing to generate the shared vision and the needed behavior changes. In our core model of a Lean management system we begin with creating clarity of purpose. In Senge's theory this leads to organizational understanding of current organizational and business reality. In some cases it can be a crisis or "burning platform" that requires changes in the organization, as shown in Figure 4.2.

The cartoon is typical of the burning platform scenario. Harvey, on the left, sees the fire and is excited. The rest of the group are acting normally, enjoying the view and unaware that their platform is on fire. The questions are: "Can Harvey warn them in time?" "Will they believe him?" and "Can they take action to save themselves?" Secondarily, "Can they save the platform or will they care?" The awakening—or call to action—can take many forms and have many different results. This could be based on technology or market shifts as well as competition with other companies, plants, or countries. We can only imagine what might have happened at Kodak if the company had begun transforming the company into digital imaging when Kodak developed it in the first place. Steven Sasson developed the first prototype which captured a black-and-white image on a digital cassette tape at a resolution of .01 megapixels in December 1975. Since then, the rise of digital imaging put an end to the film and camera industry as we knew it. While the cause of Kodak's demise seems to be the explosive nature of digital technology, it is mostly the fact that Kodak had a market position and a competence base that was rendered obsolete.

Demand for photographic films plunged in line with the growing popularity of digital cameras. In contrast, Fuji Photo implemented management reforms aimed at effecting drastic transformation of its business structures. Even as early as the 1980s, the company had foreseen the switch from film to digital, so it developed a three-pronged strategy: to squeeze as much money out of the film business as possible, to prepare for the switch to digital and to develop new business lines. While both film manufacturers recognized this fundamental change, Fuji Photo adapted to this shift much more successfully than Eastman Kodak (which filed for bankruptcy in January 2012). Fuji Photo's diversification efforts also succeeded while Kodak's had failed; furthermore Kodak built up a large but barely profitable digital camera business that was undone quickly by smartphone cameras. Such a call to action in any organization must be based on the real situation and be memorable to every member of the organization and create clarity of purpose. A simple phrase can help align company employees to action. If it's clear, no one has to wonder what they are trying to achieve and align themselves and their job as part of the overall effort. This is very simple, but also very powerful. Creating clarity of purpose starts with the customer and is constantly adapting when customer, technology, and markets change. Lean practitioners use policy deployment to guide, educate, and manage the organization's efforts. Policy deployment (Hoshin Kanri) goals are cascaded throughout the organization to the lowest levels to create awareness, urgency, and direction to drive results. This would be a prime example of clarity! The policy deployment goals come from the long-term strategy and are used to develop the company's annual plan goals. It also sets the business requirements for a management

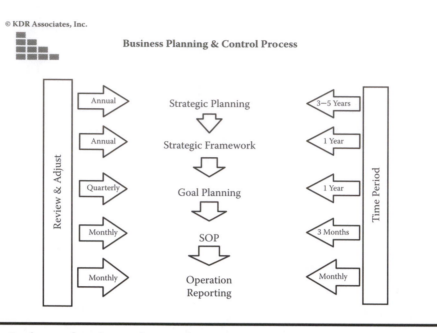

Figure 4.3   Business planning and control process.

cadence, as illustrated in Figure 4.3. There is monthly and quarterly reporting that will occur to meet both legal and managerial requirements. The board of directors will meet quarterly and review progress toward these goals, as well.

Top Management's Job

What is top management facing? Part one is to define a common vision of the current reality and the burning platform that creates a sense of urgency that changes and propels the organization. It must affect the belief system, yet offer hope for the future. Burning platforms need not be based on a crisis, but can be based on achieving new performance levels that create breakthroughs and competitive advantage.

The second part of top management's job is to help paint the view of the future. The third part is to define a pathway to achieve this view of the future, as depicted in Figure 4.4.

The role of management is to sort through the myriad possibilities, challenges, and improvements to select the few that are most important for the business to grow and prosper. Once selected, it needs to maintain focus on progress and execute effectively. The strategy deployment process is an effective way to chart the course. Figure 4.5 illustrates the path that is filled with rocks

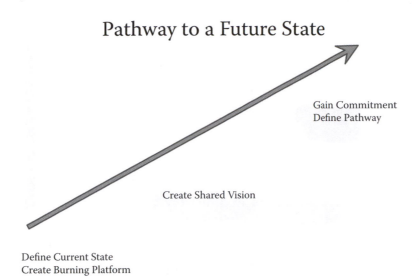

Figure 4.4 **Pathway to the future.**

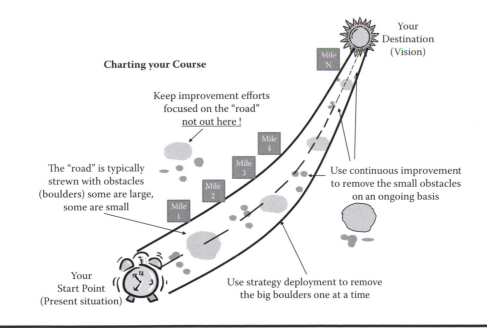

Figure 4.5 **Charting your course.**

and barriers, big and small. It also has rocks that are off path as well. A Lean strategy can be a most effective pathway. Our destination is a long-term goal, our vision, but there are barriers and milestones along the way. The milestones are set with the cadence of the business so people can see where the company is going and how the current actions remove barriers and relate to the long term.

By creating a team effort with everyone rowing in the same direction to achieve the vision, we see accelerating improvements. Too often these strategic goals are not communicated directly by management in the manner everyone can understand. Figure 4.6a shows all the elements of a strategic plan. If management can help create a shared vision of the future company per Peter Senge's model, this will play a big part in gaining acceptance and buy-in at all levels.

In Figure 4.6b, we show an example of a one-page overall strategic plan chart from Power Partners, Inc. This type of chart has been used by many companies to outline the vision, mission, core values, and drivers of change on the left side. This is the long-term vision of the company in short, crisp descriptive terms. The key result areas link to the vision and mission and define the core competencies required to achieve the vision and the performance measures to be tracked to keep the organization moving ahead. Finally, in the far right blocks are the key initiatives that the company is focusing on in the current year that contribute to achieving the long-term plan. The communication simplicity of this chart is that all levels can see the strategic plan, understand it, and identify with it! It's amazing how effective this can be in daily communications and clarity of purpose between all levels.

This type of chart was used at Texas Instruments Defense Systems and Electronics Group (DSEG) in the 1990s to be a visual guide to the path they were on and left no doubt that they were all striving for the same things and what the measures would be. This was posted in production and assembly areas, mid-managers' cubicles, and top management offices. A picture is truly worth a thousand words! In fact, one of their important customers commented, "Texas Instruments Defense was the Toyota of Defense companies!" They took this as an extreme compliment, and this culture contributed greatly to winning the 1992 Malcolm Baldrige National Quality Award—the first defense company to do so.

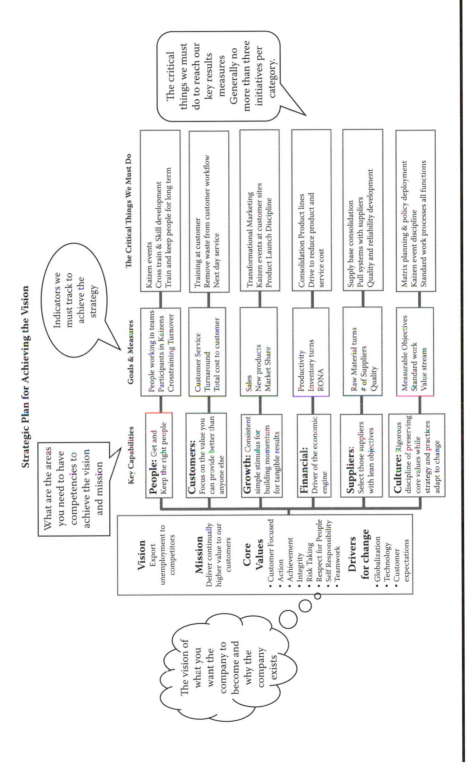

Figure 4.6a Strategy Plan.

Figure 4.6b Power Partners.

Setting Long-Term Goals

Some companies establish long-term goals that we call stretch goals, as coined by Jack Welch of General Electric (Welch, 2001). They can be based on benchmarking data, usually based on competitors' performance. One of our benchmarking peers and confidants, Melissie Rumizen,* author of *The Complete Idiot's Guide to Knowledge Management*, is quoted as saying "benchmarking is a reality check for me!" Performance data from an outside organization can be a wake-up call and be more personal and generate energy and passion and its own burning platform. GE's stretch goals can also be called Big Hairy Audacious Goals (BHAGs), a term used by Collins and Porras (1994). They defined a BHAG as "an audacious 10 to 30 year goal to progress toward an envisioned future." A BHAG is difficult, but achievable

---

* Melissie Clemmons Rumizen, *The Complete Idiot's Guide to Knowledge Management*, CWL Publishing Enterprises, Madison, WI, 2002.

Table 4.2 BHAG Opportunities

External Factors	*Internal Factors*
• Customer and market dynamics	• Customer satisfaction
• Technology shifts	• Quality
• New markets	• Delivery
• Business models	• Cost
• Supply chain	• Workforce skills

and requires cross-functional resources to execute actions and achieve. That's where management has to be smart and set the right BHAGs that truly transform the business. It may require new capabilities, products, or business models, but they affect most every part of the organization.

An effective Lean strategy will continually evaluate and set up new up-to-date BHAGs that are the basis of achieving the vision of the future company. BHAGs can be selected for the major elements of a company's target markets, products, or performance, including both external factors and internal performance, as outlined in Table 4.2.

The BHAG is usually difficult, and how to achieve it may not be clear initially. The Lean practitioners focusing on daily improvements and Kaizens most likely are inadequate to make this level of transformational change. That is what makes it a BHAG.

So then, how do we get there? We all know that hope is not a strategy, but must be tempered with the tools, people, and processes that can support the big changes in performance. This is where the Lean strategy, communicated properly, can provide this pathway to excellence and continued success. Achieving this level of change requires management and the Lean practitioners to seek nontraditional voices for input to the strategy, which would include a wider range of people in the organization, customers, suppliers, technologists, and others. The Lean practitioners and management need each other, and they need to be communicating in the same language and be attuned to the same common vision and goals.

Policy Deployment Using Catchball Communications

A BHAG will create a new future for the business, and once defined in the strategy, the most effective way to communicate down to the business managers and Lean practitioners is by an active cascading policy deployment (Hoshin Kanri) system using Catchball.

The policy deployment approach starts at the top with a company goal normally determined by the leadership team based on long-term stretch goals that are adjusted to yearly goals. It may take 2 to 3 years or longer to achieve benchmark performance. Cascading the company goals to each level of the business down to the individuals and using a fact-based interlevel negotiation process is known as the "Catchball process," where each level gets to negotiate short-term goals with management based on the learning required and barriers that need to be cleared. Achieving goals may require technology development, new skills, new equipment and capabilities, or other resources. Depending on the level of progress, goals may initially be how much have we learned from experiments run or, if in later stages, how has performance improved? This is a big step in the Lean respect for people pillar and builds commitment when fully used. The policy deployment process also applies to the current business and aligning the organization around the results required. Using the Catchball process is a key step to reducing ambiguity and misinterpretation during the planning phase to ensure that strategies, objectives, and measures are well understood, realistic, and sufficient to achieve the objectives. A BHAG will create a new future for the business and, once defined in the strategy, helps set the priorities for the year! This type of goal communication process also bonds the business leaders and the Lean practitioners to a common goal and helps set project priorities for the year! This has been used effectively by long-term Lean leaders to achieve very positive results by several companies, including Danaher, Raytheon, Texas Instruments, and others.

A good example of how policy (strategy) deployment is used in Johnson & Johnson is illustrated in Figure 4.7.

It describes its policy deployment process to communicate and cascade down all strategies, goals, and objectives to all levels of the organization as follows:

1. The company defines the overall goals of the organization, which include overall objectives, goals, strategies, and metrics for all business segments once a year for review and feedback.
2. From the business objectives, goals are given to operations plant managers once a year and reviewed every month at the business unit level. Current performance to the goals is communicated at company town hall meetings every quarter.

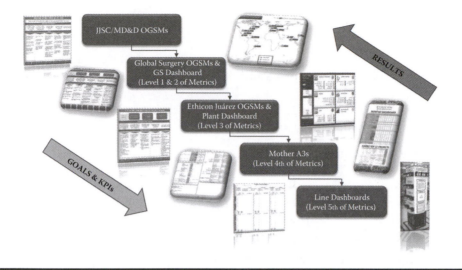

Figure 4.7 Johnson & Johnson Policy Deployment.

3. Each site develops and deploys its goals. This is fully aligned with the business and company goals. Communication of the goals is developed with site management once a year and reviewed every month at the site level. Each site has quarterly communication meetings to communicate performance to plan.

4. The sites create a visual display of the different strategic imperatives coming from the business and corporation, and progress is reviewed in weekly staff meetings.

5. From the strategy, specific metrics and goals are set and deployed to all levels of the organization down to the assembly line level.

6. Supervisors review the assembly line metrics and results at the beginning of every shift with the production line associates and they are displayed at each line dashboard.

7. Business unit (BU) metrics and results are reviewed every week in a meeting with the BU manager, manufacturing engineers (supervisors), material management representative, engineering, and quality assurance engineers.

8. Plant metrics are reviewed every week at the staff meeting.

Lean Management System

To repeat the best practice identified in Chapter 3, if top management is really serious and committed, they will incorporate the Lean strategy into

Flinchbaugh's Five Dimensions of a Business System
1. Thinking — Corporate Thoughts
2. Systems — Link all value streams and departments
3. Tools — All the Lean Tools
4. Evaluation — Benchmarking and Assessments
5. Consistency — Coordination of Dimensions 1–4

Figure 4.8 Flinchbaugh's Five Dimensions of a Business System.

the business system that we call a Lean management system, as outlined in Chapter 2, and make it "how we do work inside the company."

A Lean management system (LMS) is a strategic comprehensive system that includes all work done within the company. The LMS basically defines the culture within the company by setting a lens to be used to view company performance, opportunities, and expectations. A LMS sets the tone by structuring the thought processes, so they are consistent, transparent, and become standard work for the whole company. Companies like Danaher, Hillenbrand, and Alcoa have used their management systems to facilitate acquisitions smoothly into their corporate culture.

In Chapter 2 we outlined the core model of a Lean management system with five elements: clarity of purpose, standard work, transparency, accountability, and innovation.

Additionally, Flinchbaugh lists the five dimensions he sees in a Lean management system in Figure 4.8. It includes the overall strategic thinking, including company vision, mission, core values, and operating principles. Second, internal business systems must be created to link people and departments together while adhering to the vision, mission, values, and principles. These systems must link human resources, logistics, supply chain, manufacturing engineering, quality, finance, and all other support groups, including leadership and top management. Most of this is supported in the standard work element that defines expectations, jobs, and departments' responsibilities.

Compare Flinchbaugh's dimensions to our discussion of a Lean management model in Chapters 2 and 5:

1. Clarity of purpose → Thinking
2. Standard work → Systems and tools
3. Transparency → Systems and evaluation

4. Accountability → Evaluations and consistency
5. Innovation → Thinking and consistency

By comparison, we see many parallels to what it takes for a successful Lean management system.

The LMS must have the tools to achieve excellence in the internal systems. This is where the innovation and continuous improvement Lean tools fit in, such as value stream mapping (VSM), A3 charts, Kaizens, and all of our other favorite tools. Training of all employees and Lean practitioners is important to establishing a common language and approach to continuous improvement. The most effective way to learn is by doing what you wish to learn, so the most effective training for all employees is through their personal behavior. Emphasizing daily improvement efforts and expecting everyone to leave work each day with their work process a little better than what it was when they started the day builds and supports the common language and continuous improvement approach.

Continuous improvement, while vital, does not make strategic changes. Reevaluation must be included in the LMS to keep the current state and the future state in balance. Companies need to use benchmarking and assessments (both internal and external) to reevaluate the current reality and future state vision. External assessments such as AME's Manufacturing Excellence Award, the Shingo Prize, *Industry Week* Best Plants, and the Malcolm Baldrige National Quality Award all can give valuable feedback from an expert's perspective and provide an independent reevaluation. By looking from outside the company, a lot of perspective can be maintained. Independent eyes may see your baby as ugly—not a comfortable thought—but the reality check may be needed. Last and most important, all five of these dimensions must be coordinated and consistent to intertwine and support each other to make the Lean management system work. There will be many adjustments and improvements required as the company culture matures and develops and will need to be led by forward-thinking leaders over time. Development of the Lean management system is a top management responsibility and needs senior leadership attention on a continuing, committed basis.

In Danaher's case, the newly selected CEO to start in 2015 was instrumental in developing and teaching the Danaher Business System. For those employees in Danaher watching the culture for signals of the Lean transformation's long-term viability, this is an extremely strong signal.

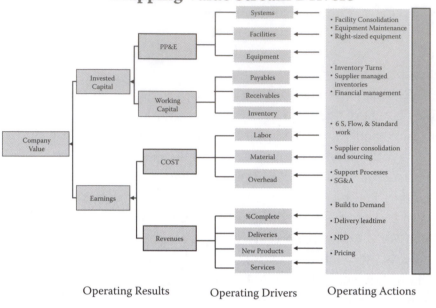

Mapping Value Stream Drivers

Figure 4.9 Mapping Value Stream Drivers.

The two pillars of Lean, continuous improvement and respect for people, which we have talked about earlier, need to be embedded in the Lean management system. Continuing communication both inside the company and to the outside world will help solidify the culture. For example, when a company refers to Lean and the management system that includes Lean in public press releases and in its annual report, this is a major signal that the Lean culture is thriving and will survive. Today we see a diverse group of companies, such as Graco, United Technologies, Danaher, and others, include Lean business systems as a key to the company's performance results in annual reports and analyst presentations. When this type of linkage is made clear, it reinforces how they support the daily work activities and how results are achieved.

As part of the business discussion, Lean practitioners and top management need to consider the value-added opportunities for the year, assign priorities, and provide resources to staff projects that move the needle to achieve the goals through policy deployment. Figure 4.9 depicts how the Lean actions link to business goals. Defining the linkage to the desired business outcome reinforces the daily work that is being done. It can become second nature and part of how work is accomplished, not something additional to the work done on a day-to-day basis.

As part of the LMS and communication, an important internal signal that top management needs to send to employees and Lean practitioners is actively "walking the talk" by going to the Gemba and coaching at different levels. This visual signal shows that top management is committed and involved and the Lean tactics and strategies are worth their time and they are in it for the long term. The bonus is that the senior management can connect with the day-to-day realities of running the business.

Another step we have witnessed in successful Lean companies is that the Lean practitioners are selected from fast-track individuals that are thought to have a bright future in the company. As mentioned earlier, currently 75% of the new CEOs are selected internally. As Lean practitioners they will learn to use the tools, interface with many levels of employees and management, and learn how to coach and mentor successors. In these companies the Lean practitioners are often on the staff of the top business manager, so they can be recognized as leading change agents that can make things happen by identifying opportunities and clearing barriers to change. In Allied Signal (now part of Honeywell), they were often already vice presidents or vice presidents-to-be. This leadership development system, driven by top management, will reinforce the Lean transformation as the fast-track/Lean practitioners are promoted and move to higher job responsibilities. This cultural norm is also a big reinforcement that the cultural transformation is for the long term.

With the Lean practitioners on the business staff, they can be part of the annual planning cycle, recognize and contribute to the business annual plan, and suggest Lean projects to directly contribute to the top manager's personal and business goals. Of course, it helps tremendously if both the top manager and the Lean practitioner are speaking the common language of business and Lean. If they form a trusted partnership, it's a win-win proposition!

Takeaways

1. Top management needs deep Lean training first!

2. Understand how key top managers and Lean practitioners use media to communicate in normal business.

3. Lean practitioners need to understand the dangers of Lean speak and use business speak when speaking to managers.

4. Lean practitioner training needs to emphasize both continuous improvement and respect for people techniques.

5. Are top managers ready to change themselves to be Lean leaders?

6. Is the company's current reality and shared vision defined and communicated regularly?

7. Does the company reevaluate its current reality through benchmarking or external assessments? And take actions to close the gap?

8. Does the company have defined stretch goals/BHAGs that are cascaded via policy deployment using catchball processes?

9. The company should define the Lean management system and continually improve it to make Lean how we do our jobs.

10. Top management sets the tone and examples by walking the talk and including Lean practitioners in the business planning discussions.

Chapter 5

What the Board Should Know about Lean

Purpose, Authority, and Responsibility of the Board of Directors

A board of directors, often simply referred to as the board, is a body of elected or appointed members who jointly oversee the activities of a company. Ask the average person as well as an investor to describe the primary responsibility of the board of directors, and very few will be able to give you a definitive answer. The same seems to hold true for employees in the typical company. Recently in a conversation with a mid-level manager who was describing the difficulty his new CEO had with the company Lean systems and how the new direction was derailing his efforts, his lament was, "Why doesn't the board do anything about the new CEO's behavior?"

While expectations of the boards have increased in the years since the Enron and WorldCom scandals, the principal role of the board of directors remains to protect the shareholders' assets and ensure they receive a decent return on their investment. The board of directors is the highest governing authority within the management structure of any publicly traded company. It is the board's job to select, evaluate, and approve appropriate compensation for the company's chief executive officer (CEO), evaluate the attractiveness of and pay dividends, recommend stock splits, oversee share repurchase programs, approve the company's financial statements, and recommend or strongly discourage acquisitions and mergers.

Typical duties of boards of directors include:

- Governing the organization by establishing broad policies and objectives
- Selecting, appointing, supporting, and reviewing the performance of the chief executive
- Ensuring the availability of adequate financial resources
- Approving annual budgets
- Accounting to the stakeholders for the organization's performance
- Setting the salaries and compensation of company management

Writers and TV commentators continue to increase expectations and lobby for boards to govern more effectively. They ask boards to set the tone from the top in promoting a transparent culture that promotes effective dialogs among the directors, senior management, various functions, and risk managers. While it is a continuing trend to pressure boards toward broader responsibilities, the purpose of an enterprise is to generate wealth. The board's job is to guide strategies and take actions that pursue profits for its stockholders.

The government still has a critical role in setting the rules of the game, and courts have affirmed the preeminence of stockholders in the for-profit corporation. Ultimately, any for-profit corporation that sells shares to others has to be accountable to its stockholders for delivering a financial return.

This is not a new notion. For those with a desire for a taste of history, consider Henry Ford's vision for Ford Motor almost 100 years ago. In a Michigan Supreme Court case, *Dodge v. Ford Motor Co.*, Henry Ford proclaimed that he was not managing Ford Motor Company to generate the best sustainable return for its stockholders. Rather, he testified that the stockholders should be content with the dividend they were getting. "My ambition," said Mr. Ford, "is to employ still more men, to spread the benefits of this industrial system to the greatest possible number, to help them build up their lives and their homes. To do this we are putting the greatest share of our profits back in the business."* Basically, the Michigan Supreme Court held that Ford could not justify his actions that way, and that although he could help other constituencies such as workers and consumers, a business corporation is organized and carried on primarily for the profit of the stockholders. The powers of the directors are to be employed for that end, and Mr. Ford could not subordinate the stockholders' best interests.

---

* *Dodge v. Ford Motor Co.*, 170 N.W. 668 (Mich. 1919).

Lest we think those times have changed, in 2010, Craigslist founders openly argued in court that they personally believe Craigslist should not be about the business of stockholder wealth maximization, now or in the future.* They were running the firm primarily to the end of something other than stockholder wealth, subordinating stockholders' financial well-being to their own unique social perspective. The Delaware Court of Chancery† ruled that a for-profit Delaware corporation, having chosen a for-profit form, is bound by fiduciary duties and standards that accompany that form. Those standards include acting to promote the value of the corporation for the benefit of its stockholders.

Finally, the board of directors does not run the day-to-day business. In fact, for clarity, we should separate the corporate enterprise from the businesses it operates. A corporation is a legal structure that enables individuals to contribute and pool resources, capital, and labor in order to generate a profit. Businesses are organizations that have customers and are the means to create value for the stakeholders: customers, employees, community, and corporation owners.

So What Do We Want the Board to Do?

Toyota, while not the largest in revenues (Volkswagen holds that honor), has become the largest automotive manufacturer in unit volume, exceeding 10 million vehicles in 2012. The Toyota Production System began to attract U.S. manufacturers' attention in the late 1970s and early 1980s. At that time, when meeting with some manufacturers and suppliers from Japan, they told us point blank, "The USA does not know how to run manufacturing."‡ One could argue that history has born that view out over the past 40 years, but that is not the point of this thesis. The real point here is that the model of business operations Toyota has developed has turned the investment in resources, capital, and people into a very attractive long-term return.

---

* *eBay Domestic Holdings Inc. v. Newmark*, 16 A.3d 1 (Del. Ch. 2010).
† The Delaware Court of Chancery is widely recognized as the nation's preeminent forum for the determination of disputes involving the internal affairs of the thousands upon thousands of Delaware corporations and other business entities through which a vast amount of the world's commercial affairs is conducted. http://courts.delaware.gov/chancery/.
‡ This was a personal discussion Ken had with a manager of a Japanese electronics manufacturer in 1973 when he was at NCR. He was the corporate supplier quality manager at the time.

What we have learned over time is the way that Toyota chose to drive for improvement in the metrics of growth, profitability, and shareholder value was through driver metrics that relate to the employee and customer, which we have illustrated in the DuPont model in Figure 1.3. The hypothesis is that if top management can drive and measure employee engagement, safety, and satisfaction, as well as quality, delivery, and innovation, superior growth and profitability will be the result. This is the essence of Lean, which we believe results in a high-quality business with a strong balance sheet, and a management team that allocates capital and works in the interest of building long-term shareholder value.

After the extreme ups and downs of financial markets during the past decade, boards of directors, senior managers, and investors need to rethink the way they define and assess corporate performance. There's nothing wrong with good accounting results and rising share prices, but they don't necessarily indicate whether a company is fundamentally healthy, in the sense of being able to sustain its current performance and build profitable businesses in the long-term future.

Nonetheless, a company can construct a comprehensive performance assessment that measures the value it has created and estimates its ability to create more. As a way of judging how well a company is doing, such an assessment is far superior to any single performance metric. It can also help management balance the short- and long-term creation of value, as well as board members and investors determine whether management's policies and the company's share price are on target.

When you participate in board meetings for companies or interact with directors, you will most likely experience a mixed message. While board members talk about people being the most important, in the end, most simply want to see the numbers. Stephen P. Kaufman in his 2008 *Harvard Business Review* article "Evaluating the CEO"* related his experience how he revised his performance evaluation process while he was at Arrow Electronics. He now is a senior lecturer at Harvard Business School, and has been a director of six public and four private companies.

Kaufman describes how after he became CEO, he was struck by how perfunctory the board was in its feedback on his performance. His article relates how the chair of the compensation committee would simply stop by his office for just 10 minutes after the year-end closed session of independent directors. The chair informed him of how the board was happy that the

---

* Stephen P. Kaufman, Evaluating the CEO, *Harvard Business Review*, October 2008, p. 53.

company had made its numbers, thanked him for his leadership, informed him what compensation it had approved, and left. His evaluation was based on a few financial measures, and the assessment was driven almost entirely by the directors' need to justify their compensation decisions.

Mr. Kaufman goes on to say that a fine line exists between counseling CEOs and telling them what to do. Directors need to give CEOs freedom to make choices. But, he adds, to use CEO autonomy as an argument for limiting performance management to only financial measures makes little sense. All the incentives in the world won't transform CEOs into better decision makers. And when CEOs stumble or fall, they pull their companies down with them. Boards have an obligation to shareholders to ensure that companies are led well, and the sooner they can spot problems with leaders' performance, the better. As it is, by the time companies fire or hire the new CEOs, the damage has already been done.

Toyota has taught us that leaders cannot lead unless they have the respect of their people and have respect for people. This yin and yang of leadership cannot be developed or described if the CEO is only evaluated by financials. To do a better job of giving feedback to a CEO, the board needs to spend more time talking to executives and observing operations and the health of the organizational culture. Only then can they be aware of, detect, and give advice on how to fix problems the CEO may have missed—before the issues escalate into disasters.

In his article Mr. Kaufman proposed that the CEO evaluation process address the following key areas:

1. Leadership. How well does the CEO motivate and energize the organization, and is the company's culture reinforcing its mission and values?
2. Strategy. Is it working, is the company aligned behind it, and is it being effectively implemented?
3. People management. Is the CEO putting the right people in the right jobs, and is there a stream of appropriate people for succession and to support growth goals? (We would add: Is there a system in place to develop people and leaders?)
4. Operating metrics. Are sales, profits, productivity, asset utilization, quality, and customer satisfaction heading in the right direction?
5. Relationships with external constituencies. How well does the CEO engage with the company's customers, suppliers, and other stakeholders?

GM Board Committees

- Audit Committee
- Compensation Committee
- Governance Committee
- Finance Committee
- Public Policy Committee

In a recent discussion with Mr. Kaufman, he related that most public companies continue with solely the financials approach and estimates that only 30 to 35% of the company boards are following a broader evaluation approach such as he described above. In addition, he suggests that today he would advise board members to put more emphasis on the operations side. We would add putting greater emphasis on the corporate culture development in the business.

One of the essential functions of the board is oversight of management, directly and through its various committees or director assignments. However, depending on the issue or the company's situation, the role of the board can switch from overseer to active participant. When boards are more actively involved, it is typically in the areas of financial audit, strategy, and CEO succession, rather than operations and sales. According to GM's 2014 proxy statement, for example, the GM board has five board committees assigned to keep tabs on risk-related issues, but none seem specifically responsible for operational risks, including organizational culture. We suggest this is a serious board shortcoming, as culture more often than not trumps strategy, as we mentioned in Chapter 4. It is the culture of the organization that influences how the company executes its mission. The headlines referencing GM in June and July 2014, addressing the investigation into the ignition switch recall referenced in Chapter 1, highlight this shortcoming. The company internal probe reported a corporate culture characterized by departmental isolation and lack of transparency and accountability as the root cause of the automaker's 11-year failure to deal with cars equipped with a defective ignition switch. Had the board considered corporate culture a risk-related issue and made a practice of interacting with the organization on a regular basis, it could have directed the company to address this before the performance issues became a public crisis.

Organizational Alignment

While there's no cookbook checklist to follow, board members and executive management should agree on how involved the board will be in key areas. Board members can begin by asking themselves: "How do we execute our fiduciary responsibilities while continuing to support the company management and their strategies?" The answer to that question lies in examining the company's management system for how the organization is practicing the five elements of the core management model described in Chapter 2. Fundamentally, the board members should look for organization alignment around the company strategy, mission, and core values. Work processes that people follow, especially problem solving, should be clearly understood. Information should be clearly available throughout the organization, and people should have access to the information regarding the company and the jobs they are assigned. People need to feel they are accountable for the success of the company in carrying out its mission and for its target customers, regardless of the department or job title they have. Finally, the organization should be in continual transformation and improvement. The organization needs to have a healthy dissatisfaction with the status quo. Satisfaction with the current business status cannot be tolerated.

Companies will come to lots of crossroads along the way. Sometimes the path chosen will cause the company to falter, and perhaps fail. In times of crisis or market fluctuation, the board may need to be more engaged in helping management create solutions. Board members, drawing upon their expertise, contacts, and experience, can help the company management avoid fatal steps in making the proper decisions. Interaction between the board and the management beyond the board meetings is encouraged to provide forums to review issues, share experiences, discuss and evaluate the alternatives, and come to appropriate conclusions.

Core Management Model

- Clarity of purpose
- Standard work
- Transparency
- Accountability
- Innovation

By themselves, accounting and financial reports do not adequately tell the story of how the company is doing. Nonfinancial metrics are equally or more important in terms of updating the board on company progress. This is where the culture and driver metrics come into play, and what the board should be looking for in order to anticipate future issues and prepare for them. The board should see the trajectory of the company's progress in product development, sales, business development, operations, and organizational and people development to identify the areas that do, or will, need bolstering. The board of a manufacturing company, for example, should look at trends in order cycle times, inventory turns, customer experience, and employee engagement. Better yet, the board of directors should go to the customer interaction points and the production floor, talk with the people, and participate in improvement activities. Going to the action where work takes place, what we call Gemba, is where one develops a real understanding of how the company is creating value.

Does the Board Set the Company Culture?

The term *company culture* gets tossed around a lot. For many it is synonymous with the "touchy-feely, soft stuff" and the idea of shucking traditional corporate bureaucracy to optimize happiness and creativity. Others describe it as the personality of a company and define what a company is like to work for from an employee perspective. Culture therefore is the group norms of behavior and the underlying shared values, including standards and moral codes, that help keep those norms in place. We are not talking about free food, on-site fitness centers, and massages as an indicator of a great company culture. For our discussion we will use a simple definition: a "good" culture is one that supports the company's business strategy and recognizes that operating a business is an endeavor with varying degrees of uncertainty. Sometimes it is smooth sailing (that's when you should really worry that something is about to change; like the stock market, when everyone is happy and confident, that is when the bottom falls out), and other times it is a nail-biter. Nonetheless, our definition of culture is how real work is done to add value and drive performance. This is made visible in the company with its vision, mission, and values, how it sets expectations, displays trust, and engages its people in problem solving, idea sharing, promoting innovation, etc. If free food and massages are included, that's OK too.

So our question about company culture is: Does the board set the culture? The answer is yes, but indirectly. An organization's success is, in large part, driven by how wisely it takes risks and how effectively it manages the risks it faces. The enterprise's culture comes into play here because people tend to do what they are rewarded to do. We believe the board sets the culture when selecting, evaluating, and compensating the CEO. The board sets the tone of the organization's risk culture in the business strategy it supports. For example, the board's action regarding Company X in Chapter 2 certainly set in motion a significant culture change. While we do not know why their succession planning, or lack of it, failed to produce a successor internally, the board elected to go outside of the company to fill the CEO position. Subsequently, the new CEO initiated changes in the management system to a more authoritative and financially driven model, which had a domino effect in the organization and resulted in destroying the culture of engaged people established for over 12 years.

It's important to think through all potential implications—intentional and unintentional—of executive rewards to make sure the board is encouraging people to take risks intelligently. Similarly, the board should also understand how incentive programs implemented throughout the organization may influence the risk culture below the C-suite. Why encourage risk taking? What a Lean culture does is support hands-on contributors who embrace and drive change. The power is derived from the collective knowledge and brainpower of the organization. Consider for a moment the pricing power that the Ritz Carlton has vs. Motel 6. While each is targeting a different clientele, the Ritz could not sustain its business model for 100 years without engaged employees aligned to the business strategy with a corporate philosophy of unwavering commitment to service. Their empowered employees have an individual responsibility to see customers are taken care of, including the individual ability to spend cash to see that it happens! It has been recognized with numerous awards for being the gold standard of hospitality. Motel 6 would not have sustained its 50 years of economy lodging without having the employees aligned with their product strategy: "lowest price of any national chain," i.e., good value at low cost. The companies are targeting different market segments, but both are striving for well-managed properties with satisfied guests.

Extinction Is an Option

The last dinosaurs died approximately 65 million years ago. Although the cause of their extinction is still a subject of much debate and controversy, climatic change, diseases, changing plant communities, and geologic events could all have played a role. Regardless of the details, most of the theories share in common the thought that dinosaurs were a group of animals that had reached the end of their evolutionary life. Their extinction is seen as inevitable, and in most theories, the dinosaurs were simply unable to cope with competition from mammals and the changing climate. Interestingly, operating a business has very similar issues.

The United States has always been the land of opportunity, giving any citizen the right to start a business and grow it as large as his or her dreams can take him or her. Some years have been better than others, and the risks of starting a business can be high, but the rewards can be well worth it. With over a half million new businesses starting each year, and almost an equal amount closing, the economy needs new fresh ideas from entrepreneurs to help carry it through the next decade.[*]

The recent bankruptcy of Eastman Kodak[†] (August 23, 2013) reminds us that even the largest businesses do not live forever. While the Standard & Poor's 500 index has been around since March 1957 (see appendix for the original S&P 500 list), the makeup of the index itself has undergone dramatic changes, as companies have been added and subtracted because of mergers, acquisitions, and other changes in company fortunes. Our study of the S&P 500 index found that 65 companies (S&P 500 Survivors List) that were on the original list have survived their 57-year anniversary as of March 2014. Additionally, studies and reports in business journals have found the life spans of top U.S. companies to be shrinking. Companies struggle with the pace of global competition, changing technology, and pressure from start-ups, including some of the most iconic corporations, such as we have seen with Kodak.

---

[*] Small Business Association, U.S. Department of Labor.

[†] Upon emergence from Chapter 11, Kodak applied the provisions of fresh-start accounting to its financial statements as of September 1, 2013. Adoption of fresh-start accounting resulted in Kodak becoming a new entity for financial reporting purposes. Accordingly, the consolidated financial statements on or after September 1, 2013, are not comparable to the consolidated financial statements prior to that date.

S&P 500 Survivors

S&P 500 Companies since 1957	
3M (MMM)	Goodyear Tire & Rubber (GT)
Abbott Laboratories (ABT)	Halliburton (HAL)
Alcoa (AA)	Hartford Financial Services (HIG)
Allstate (ALL)	Hershey (HSY)
Altria Group (MO)	Honeywell International (HON)
American Electric Power (AEP)	IBM (IBM)
Archer Daniels Midland (ADM)	Ingersoll-Rand (IR)
Boeing (BA)	International Paper (IP)
Bristol-Myers Squibb (BMY)	Kimberly-Clark (KMB)
Campbell Soup (CPB)	Kroger (KR)
Caterpillar (CAT)	Lockheed Martin (LMT)
Chevron (CVX)	Marathon Oil (MRO)
CMS Energy (CMS)	MeadWestvaco (MWV)
Coca-Cola (KO)	Merck (MRK)
Colgate-Palmolive (CL)	Norfolk Southern (NSC)
ConocoPhillips (COP)	Northrop Grumman (NOC)
Consolidated Edison (ED)	Occidental Petroleum (OXY)
CSX (CSX)	PepsiCo (PEP)
CVS (CVS)	Pfizer (PFE)
Deere (DE)	PG&E (PCG)
Dow Chemical (DOW)	Pitney Bowes (PBI)
DTE Energy (DTE)	PPG Industries (PPG)
DuPont (DD)	Procter & Gamble (PG)
Eaton (ETN)	Quest Diagnostics (DGX)
Edison International (EIX)	Raytheon (RTN)
Entergy (ETR)	Rockwell Collins (COL)
Exelon (EXC)	Schlumberger (SLB)

Exxon Mobil (XOM)	Sealed Air (SEE)
Ford Motor (F)	Southern Co. (SO)
General Dynamics (GD)	Union Pacific (UNP)
General Electric (GE)	United Technologies (UTX)
General Mills (GIS)	Xcel Energy (XEL)
General Motors (GM)	

What is consistent about the surviving companies from the 1957 list is they have so far continued to keep up with the changes the company has encountered over the years. As a contrast to Kodak, an iconic company still operating today is NCR, although not on the 2014 S&P 500 listing. Originally named National Cash Register, NCR was founded in 1884 and was the market leader for mechanical cash registers for years. Responding to changing customer expectations and technology drove the company through numerous transformations throughout the years. Today NCR is a global tech company in consumer transaction technologies and everyday interactions with businesses. Reviewing the NCR timeline at the end of this chapter, you will see the company has gone through many changes over the past 130 years. While keeping its focus on its target customers, NCR adjusted its products and services as well as its resources to respond to continually changing technology and customer expectations. It is not the same company it was when founded in 1884.

While it is clear that all companies will have to adapt to change, most do not. Less than 50% of businesses survive beyond 5 years, and only a small minority (13%) of the S&P 500 companies have managed to survive since 1957 through the many changes in technology, regulations, competitors, customer dynamics, and the world economic environment. The Austrian-American economist Joseph Schumpeter (1883–1950) studied the formation and bankruptcy of companies in Europe and the United States. He concluded that economic progress, in capitalist society, means turmoil and coined the term *creative destruction*. Richard Foster and Sarah Kaplan, in their book *Creative Destruction,*[*] applied Schumpeter's theory to the modern

---

[*] Richard Foster and Sarah Kaplan, *Creative Destruction: Why Companies That Are Built to Last Underperform the Market—And How to Successfully Transform Them*, Doubleday, New York, 2001.

practices of management with the impact of innovation and have postulated a few key macro characteristics that can help companies last through the long haul.

According to Foster and Kaplan, the life span of a corporation is determined by balancing three management imperatives: (1) running operations effectively, (2) creating new businesses that meet customer needs, and (3) shedding business that once might have been core, but now no longer meets company standards for growth and return. What these findings suggest is that companies need to be continuously transforming to create the organizational flexibility to accomplish these imperatives. In other words, sustainment is a myth and transformation is a requirement!

Corporations operate with management philosophies based on the assumption of continuity, which makes change and value creation at the pace of the marketplace difficult. The control processes used to meet quarterly and annual numbers anesthetize them and separate them from the vital and constant requirement for change. In going back to the origins of the Toyota Production System, our predecessor to Lean, survival was a key motivator. The principles that kept it alive at that time has kept Toyota in a growth mode ever since. The customer focus proposition of Lean provides the guide for the dynamic strategies of driving change in products and processes, which must be adopted in order to remain relevant and competitive in the marketplace.

We propose using Lean as a strategy, not as a process improvement methodology or set of tools to do something in a different way. *In other words, use Lean to differentiate your company to your customers, rather than simply using it as a way to clean up the shop.*

Lean starts with the customer and the market that the company is targeting to serve. The board should challenge the CEO and the management team to develop and align their organizations to overcome stagnation by transforming for the future as well as incrementally improving their companies. Organizations can accomplish this by clear connection with customers and roadmapping technologies that lead to creating new products, services, and businesses to become more responsive to the market. What is required is adopting flexible decision-making processes, control systems, and mental models. In doing so, they must take action to creatively deal with businesses or divisions whose growth is slowing down, as well as abandoning outdated technologies, bureaucratic structures, and policies. This approach broadens the prevailing practice of focusing on simple incremental adjustments that improve current business performance that we see with Kaizen events and continuous improvement programs to a more holistic transformation process. Corporations, we suggest, accomplish this with Lean as an overall organizational strategy, not just by implementing some Lean methods in operations.

What a Lean Strategy Does

Corporations are designed to create value, or should be. In a Lean strategy that value is defined by what the customer is willing to pay for and nothing else. It is a difficult metric in that any activity, investment, or initiative needs to be held up to the high standard: Will the customer be willing to pay for this? This is a tough standard to follow; consequently, most just do not ask the question. Our goal here is not to be critical of what companies do, but to provide an illustration of what a Lean strategy can do for a company. Asking the question creates opportunities for companies. In this discussion, to illustrate a Lean strategy across a business, we have pulled real cases from different companies as examples into one company. This amalgam of companies we will use for illustration of transformation actions we will name Amalgam, Inc., or Amalgam for short. The situations are real and so are the results shown.

Amalgam Business Context

Amalgam designs, manufactures, and markets products and services, which are typically characterized in the marketplace by strong brand names and innovative technology with major market positions. Its research and development, manufacturing, sales, distribution, service, and administrative facilities are located in a number of countries around the world. Its business consists of multiple segments, and it is striving to create shareholder value by delivering revenue and profit growth at an annual rate greater than the average of the Fortune 100, or greater than 8%.

Over the years it has grown slowly with its markets and enhanced its growth rate with acquired businesses that it believed either strategically fit within its existing business portfolio or allowed it to expand into new business areas it found attractive. Amalgam can be characterized as a medium-sized global company with a large variety of products, redundant and complex organizational structure, and multitudes of processes that create internal confusion, which sometimes frustrates its customers. The impact of Amalgam's strategy created growth (mostly through acquisitions), but the profitability has been a struggle, leading it to employ a number of "right sizing" and other cost reduction programs with disappointing results. It should not be a surprise, since a cost reduction strategy that focuses on doing things the same way, but cheaper, is likely to lead to disappointing results.

The takeaway here is that cost reduction programs have rarely worked to build shareholder value over the long term because they do not address the holistic problem. In contrast, activities such as transformative marketing and new products that create customer value and responsive operations turn into top-line growth and profitability. It is our assertion that the best path to this goal is using a Lean strategy to focus on customer value creation by attacking the organizational, product, and process issues that create the barriers to value creation. To do that, the CEO and his management team need to assess and analyze the non-value-adding activities to create understanding of the size of the opportunity for improvement, choose the right focus, and align the company around the direction of the business. This analysis should be holistic and expressed in terms of financial impact, the performance drivers impacted, and a strategy to address them. These are, most often, not currently addressed at the board level, but should be since this will provide the basis for aligning the company strategy.

Consider our example company, Amalgam, whose growth strategy has been through acquisition. The collective acquisitions created growth without capitalizing effectively on the synergies by integrating the acquired businesses. The company ended up with multiple locations, and duplication of management and functional organizations because of the number of locations. Product lines and SKUs multiplied, presenting customers with many alternate products and sometimes confusing options. Margins have been supported with cost reductions, but have declined slightly, and customer service has suffered.

The management analysis might be as follows:

1. Financial impact: Financially quantify the size of the non-value-added activity resources currently deployed in the company. Generally accepted accounting principles (GAAP) systems are not designed to capture these costs, so they are hidden from view. Even when costs become recognized, it is difficult to put a financial number on the non-value-adding costs. We can, however, provide initial estimates that gauge relative impact and guide the direction of actions to take.

   By analyzing their non-value-added activities and products, Amalgam found two significant opportunities:

a. The multiplication of locations created complex and redundant management structures, adding millions in cost as well as creating competing demand for capital, operations, sales, and R&D resources.

b. Product proliferation was counterproductive. Products did not create demand, but cannibalized each other, reducing the economies of scale for materials and manufacturing. While normal standard cost indicated that almost all products yielded some margin, 24% of the product lines contributed 95% of the company profit (Figure 5.1). Further analysis of products found that as many as 50% of the product lines were adding little revenue, and actually subtracting from overall company profit.

2. Performance drivers: Once the non-value-added activity is quantified, it will most likely be large. The scale of focus and drivers will need to be defined. The cross-functional effort required to address the issues requires organizational functions to work together; otherwise, these efforts will be reduced to piecemeal efforts that yield few results. Identifying the few driver metrics that the organization will use to guide actions will create better focus. Depending on the focus of the efforts needed, these will be different.

Selecting the right performance drivers requires answering the question "What needle are you trying to move?" In Amalgam's case, it is seeking to capitalize on the acquisition growth and synergies to improve profitability and company value. Using the DuPont analysis (Figure 1.3) from Chapter 1 to select the key drivers for improvement illustrated in Figure 5.2, the drivers can be identified and measures established. The driver areas are in three areas, suggesting that Amalgam will drive to move the needle in service, administrative overhead, inventory, and fixed asset turns. We suggest limiting the number of drivers to one customer-related driver and no more than three internal drivers to keep the focus.

3. Organizational strategy: Even companies that understand the financial opportunity and have identified the drivers can get stuck. Analysis paralysis that frequently stalls the best intentions of organizations can delay or prevent any meaningful action. What is needed is a simple A3 to describe a plan that is appropriate to the nature of the target, such as the one in Figure 5.3.

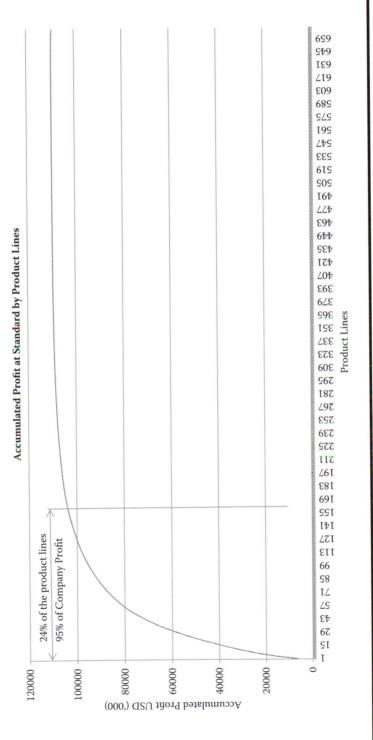

Figure 5.1 Accumulated profit at standard by product lines.

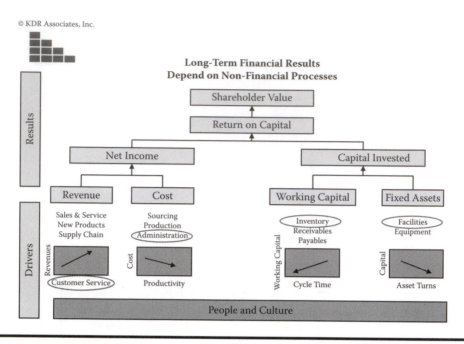

Figure 5.2   Key drivers.

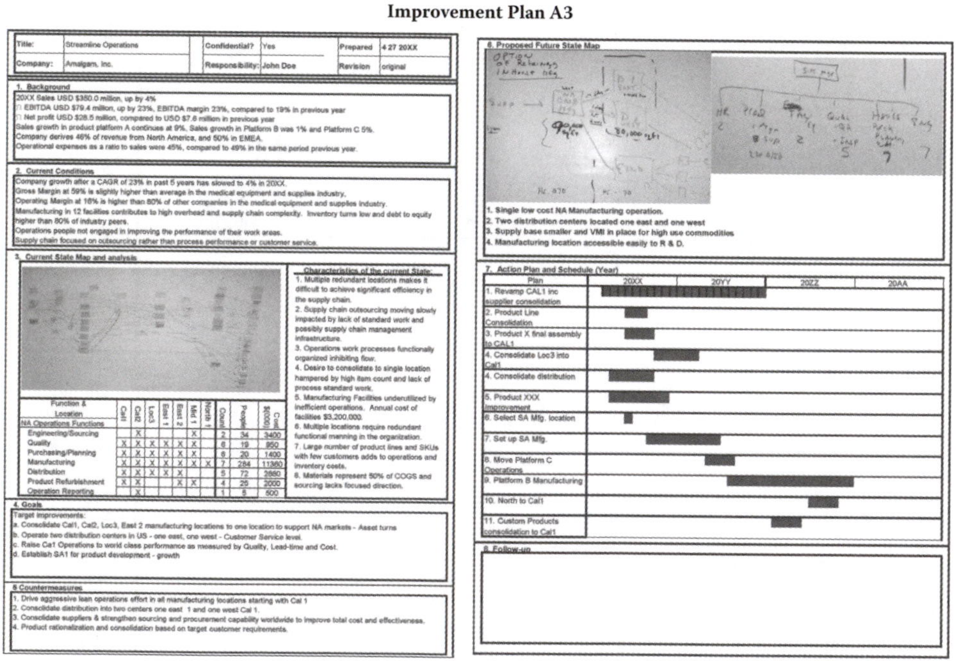

Improvement Plan A3

Figure 5.3   Improvement plan A3.

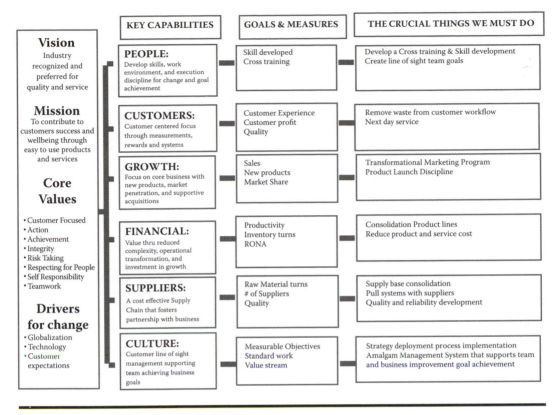

Figure 5.4   Amalgam strategic framework.

Amalgam decided to use and adapt the strategic framework introduced in Chapter 4 Figure 4.5. The work they did to align their management team to the strategy and develop the management cadence to drive implementation is illustrated in Figure 5.4. In later chapters we will further examine these three dimensions using our example company, Amalgam. We will illustrate how to financially define the opportunity, select appropriate performance drivers, and keep the focus on the goal. We will also suggest ways to engage the organization with a leadership cadence that takes action to successfully remove the non-value-added activity and create greater value for the business stakeholders (customers, employees, shareholders).

Takeaway Questions to Consider for Your Company

1. Does the board have a practice of interacting with the operating groups in the company? _____

2. Are performance drivers and trends part of the management review process? _____

3. What is the company transformation plan to adapt to the future? _____
   _____

4. Have the performance gaps been defined? _____

5. Has the transformation plan been communicated to the organization appropriately? _____

NCR Timeline*

1884: John H. Patterson founded the National Cash Register Company, maker of the first mechanical cash registers.

1893: NCR opened the first sales training school.

1906: Charles F. Kettering designed the first cash register powered by an electric motor.

1914: NCR developed one of the first automated credit systems.

1926: NCR became publicly owned.

1952: NCR acquired Computer Research Corporation (CRC) of Hawthorne, California, which produced a line of digital computers with applications in aviation.

1953: NCR established the Electronics Division to continue to pursue electronic applications for business machines.

1957: NCR announced the first fully transistorized business computer, the NCR 304.

1968: NCR's John L. Janning perfected liquid crystal displays (LCDs).

1974: Company changed its name to NCR Corporation.

1974: NCR commercialized the first bar code scanners.

---

* http://www.ncr.com/about-ncr/company-overview/history-timeline.

1982: The first NCR Tower supermicrocomputer system was launched, establishing NCR as a pioneer in bringing industry standards and open systems architecture to the computer market.

1991: NCR acquired by AT&T.

1991: NCR purchased Teradata Corporation, acquiring its advanced and unique commercial parallel processing technology. NCR Teradata becomes the world's most proven and powerful database for data warehousing.

1994: NCR name changed to AT&T Global Information Solutions (GIS).

1995: AT&T announced spin-off of AT&T GIS by the end of 1996.

1996: AT&T GIS changed its name back to NCR Corporation in anticipation of being spun off to AT&T shareholders by January 1997, as an independent, publicly traded company.

1997: Signaling its evolution from a hardware-only company to a full solutions provider, NCR purchased Compris Technologies, Inc., a leading provider of store automation and management software for the food service industry, and Dataworks, a company that develops check processing software.

1998: NCR finalized the transfer and sale of its computer hardware manufacturing assets to Solectron, confirming NCR's commitment to concentrate on the market-differentiated software and services components of its solutions portfolios.

2000: NCR acquired CRM provider Ceres Integrated Solutions and services company 4Front Technologies, deepening NCR's solutions offerings in key markets.

2003: NCR granted patent for signature capture.

2005: Following the successful 2004 acquisition of travel self-service leader Kinetics, NCR further strengthens its self-service portfolio by acquiring Galvanon, a leading provider of solutions for the healthcare industry.

2007: NCR separated into two companies through the spin-off of the Teradata data warehousing business.

2009: NCR establishes its new corporate headquarters in Duluth, Georgia.

2010: NCR introduces industry's first mixed media deposit ATMs (Scalable Deposit Module (SDM)).

2011: NCR completes $1 billion acquisition of Radiant Systems, expanding NCR's presence in the hospitality and specialty retail spaces.

2012: NCR launches NCR Silver, a cloud-based point of sale system for small businesses.

2013: NCR completes $650 million acquisition of Retalix, adding innovative retail software and services.

2014: NCR completes $1.65 billion acquisition of Digital Insight, providing a market leading software as a service (SaaS) platform to help banks transform their physical and digital business models.

Chapter 6

Using Your Lean Culture to Achieve the CEO's Goals

Lean thinking is energetic, no-holds-barred thinking!

"I'm open to change and I'm here to make a difference."

This type of thinking is a radical departure from the historical worker thinking of "I'm here to do what I'm told and I use my brain outside of work in family affairs and community activities, but not at work." Lean thinking challenges everyone to be the manager of their own actions, by challenging "This is how we do things here" and the ever-popular "If it ain't broke, don't fix it!" After all, all processes can be improved by using new technology and eliminating unnecessary steps that may have been needed in the past. The world does change, and the spoils go to the company that adapts rapidly and takes advantage of the new conditions.

In Jim Womack and Dan Jones's book *Lean Thinking*, we are reminded that there are five key high-level principles of a Lean system:

1. Precisely specify value by specific product.
2. Identify the value stream for each product.
3. Make value flow without interruption.
4. Let the customer pull value from the producer.
5. Pursue perfection.

Based on their 15 years of benchmarking, Womack and Jones conclude that converting a classic batch and queue (push system) to a continuous flow (pull system) with pull by the customer will double productivity of all employees (workers, managers, engineers, support people) and reduce cycle times by 90% and inventories by 90%! Adding to this, defects are typically reduced 50%, job-related injuries are cut in half, and product development times to market times are also halved!* This initially gave rise to our focus on learning how to use specific tools that appeared to be the Holy Grail and tool of the month approach in many companies. Many companies became very good at using 5S, Poka-Yoke, value srteam mapping, teams, cells, Just-in-Time, Kaizens, and so on.

The trick is how to combine all these tools into the company culture on a daily basis under the five key principles stated above, which are based on the two main Lean building blocks: continuous improvement and respect for people. Toyota itself did not publicize that these were the tools of an overall company approach to business; in its case, this was an assumed understanding of how it did work. Jeffrey Liker's book *The Toyota Way*, published in 2004,† became the reference of how this set of tools is integrated into Toyota's daily work and culture, but this was 25 years after many companies had tried the tools as a cost-cutting approach. Some of our examples in Lean for the long term identify companies that understand the importance of Lean as a business system and culture which we will highlight in this chapter: Danaher, Autoliv, Hillenbrand, and Ford, for example.

Worker Engagement

Most employees are not fully engaged at work. So a big advantage is that a Lean management system, properly deployed, is a tremendous lever to have everyone be a manager of their own activities. In a Lean management system, they are taught to challenge everything and eliminate non-value-added activities and steps in the value stream process. Ask yourself, "If the customer won't pay for it, why are we doing it?" This sounds simple, but strategically, it has ramifications across the whole company and in all departments and product lines. Too often in the bureaucracy of an organization there are defensive additions made to the business processes, products, and services that add cost, cycle time, and are of little customer value. The additions may protect a department from critique, but that is not value added from a customer

---

* James P. Womack and Daniel T. Jones, *Lean Thinking*, Free Press, New York, 2003, pp. 10, 27.
† Jeffrey K. Liker, *The Toyota Way*, McGraw-Hill, New York, 2004.

standpoint, and they would not pay for it! By promoting Lean principles and expecting assumptions to be challenged along each step in the process, the engagement of all workers can be solicited and better long-term job satisfaction can be generated.

Lean Culture and the CEO's Strategy

So how do we translate this Lean strategy and the use of all the principles and tools to a management-friendly language, i.e., management or financial speak? A most common and simplistic way to measure value generated by employees is by the metric of productivity and a simple financial definition is:

$$Productivity = Revenue/Employees$$

How much revenue is generated per person? Comparison with your industry is most relevant and adds an apples-to-apples benchmark. High-tech and knowledge worker-centered companies will have higher revenue-to-employee ratios. The major factors and dependencies on this generalized productivity measure are many, including industry, labor content vs. material, and technology involved and the business model, but it is a good quick thumbnail way to analyze relative value added. The business model can include operations outsourced, so comparisons need to be aware of this factor as well. In Figure 6.1[*] you will note that Apple has by far the highest ratio of over $2 million per employee, and IBM is at about $230,000 per employee, or about eight times less value per employee.

What this ratio means is that everyone in the organization needs to pull their own weight. Each person, employee, or team member is responsible for contributing to the products and services that the customers are paying for. This is also a basic concept of Lean's value-added quest. Each activity in the company should be questioned to determine if it is value added or not. Lots of things become ingrown after years—different bosses, organization changes, and programs of the month. That's the beauty of Lean management—to challenge everything as the real world changes. The CEO is the overall single person responsible to all stakeholders: stockholders, employees, and customers. Of course, he or she has lots of help, but it is the CEO's strategy that will be evaluated by the financial community in terms of company value and stockholder value.

---

[*] *Fortune*, 1st quarter, 2014.

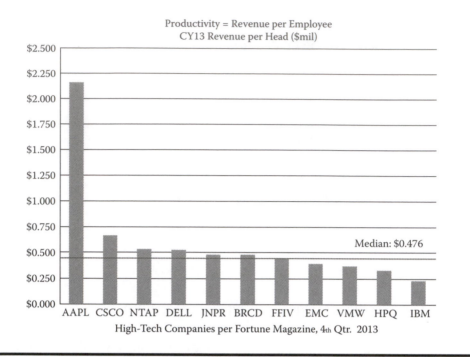

Figure 6.1   Productivity = Revenue per employee.

- Analysts and Wall Street investors look at their own interests and their own direct stockholders' interests and measure company value based on stock price on a minute-by-minute basis, and usually quarterly and yearly results are treated as major milestones of value of the company.
- Customers are generally measured by sales volume and returning customers. Typical measures are same store sales, number of users, unit volume sold, etc.
- Employees are much trickier, but some indicators are ideas generated, turnover, innovations, patents, and participation on teams.

A Lean management strategy addresses all three of these stakeholders in positive terms and can be a very valuable tool of the CEO as he considers where the opportunities are to apply his time and resources. The CEO is trying to add value by growing the top line and increasing bottom-line profitability to the bottom-line profitability with the most effective approach and the fastest long-term solutions. Unfortunately, fastest and long-term approaches may be in conflict, and the CEO must balance the strategy to achieve both. As mentioned in Chapter 5, the board should be evaluating the balance between the two since their basic job is to protect the shareholders' interests.

As a CEO, we've mentioned one of the performance metrics is the stock price, which is often part of his or her compensation package, beginning when he or she took over as CEO and what has happened during his or her tenure. Let's look at some current examples of companies that have adopted a Lean management strategy and their long-term results.

Ford Motor Company

Recently, Alan Mulally, CEO of Ford Motor Company, has announced his retirement in mid-2014. So what is his legacy and achievement in the performance metrics arena? Since he took over in 2006 until mid-2014, the price of Ford's stock price has nearly doubled and has recognized a profit in 19 consecutive quarters by using its business strategy called One Ford Plan. By these measures the CEO has been successful and has exceeded expectations, as Ford came through the 2007–2008 economic recession without the government assistance required by General Motors and Chrysler. Mulally, in his retirement announcement, said he has nothing left to teach his successor, COO Mark Fields.* From the news report referenced below, we can summarize the financial analyst's interpretation of the value he brought to the company since September 2006: the One Ford Plan, the share price growth based on restructuring and developing new products, and confidence that the management team is ready for the transition now.

We can take this as our roadmap on what the successful CEO thinks are his major goals:

1. A strategic business plan that pulls everyone in the right direction and that the company employees, including management, are aligned to achieve mutual goals and aspirations
2. Increasing stock price, which is usually based on stable profits and good profit expectations, all based on creating customer value
3. Succession planning for the continuous improvement culture, as well as the CEO successor that is steeped in the culture

In Figure 6.2 we can see how these principles are embedded in the One Ford Plan.

The One Team definition is explained clearly as "people working together as a lean, global enterprise for automotive leadership" as measured by

---

* Mathew Rocco, Fox Business News, May 1, 2014.

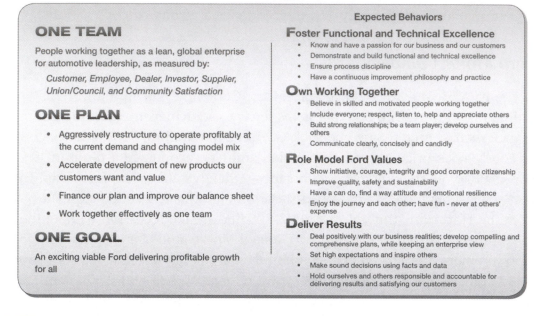

Figure 6.2 One Ford.

all stakeholders' satisfaction. This makes it abundantly clear that they are expecting Lean operations in all areas of the company.

Over in the expected behaviors section they list:

- Ensure process discipline
- Have a continuous improvement philosophy and practice
- Build strong relationships; be a team player; develop ourselves and others
- Have a "can do, find a way" attitude and emotional resilience
- Set high expectations and inspire others
- Make sound decisions using facts and data

These elements are all building blocks to a successful Lean enterprise, and we see Ford defining the cultural expectations up front, so that all employees will continually see the Lean management system (LMS) communications and the One Ford Plan and believe it is here to stay. This is very important to a company that is Ford's size and the many locations and products and services.

Hillenbrand, Inc.

If you are not familiar with Hillenbrand, it is a 100-year-old industry leader that has been implementing a Lean philosophy since 1995. In 2007 Batesville Casket Company and Hill-Rom, a medical device supplier of hospital beds and equipment, split into separate companies. Batesville on April 1, 2008, became the major portion of Hillenbrand Industries. It is using its strategy, which features Lean as a keystone, to improve the company while bringing four growth acquisitions online. Let's look at the Batesville business unit, which features the Batesville Casket Company. The Batesville Casket Company has won *Industry Week* Best Plant Awards in 2006, 2009, and 2010 and an AME Manufacturing Excellence Award in 2011, and is the driving element of its continuous improvement and Lean philosophy that has been deployed companywide. In a slow growth market, with more funerals turning to less expensive cremations and the baby boomer population cresting, it has actively used the Lean strategy to create customer and shareholder value. Since 2009, the overall company's cap value has increased from $1.2 billion to $1.9 billion, a 58% increase, and its gross profit margin has increased to 35.99%. Stock price has risen from 1Q 2008 of $22.10 per share to $29.86 as of May 8, 2014, an increase of 35%. These financial accomplishments have contributed greatly to meet the CEO's goals of growth and joining new markets. Batesville Casket was the basis of the company until 2009, when management determined that its future was best addressed by acquiring companies in growth markets. Using its "relentless focus on Lean" approach[*] and leveraging the stable and profitable Batesville Casket as its cash engine, it was able to acquire four businesses in the process equipment industry; the acquisitions were Coperion, Coperion K-Tron, Rotex, and TerraSource Global. In 2013 revenue, Batesville Casket was at $621 million and the acquired process companies contributed almost $1 billion, so Batesville is, as of mid-2014, now about 40% of Hillenbrand, indicating the business model transformation was well underway. The new business model was becoming successful. The company is alert and aware of the effect of changing markets, opportunities, and technology, as mentioned in Chapter 5.

In its strategy graphic it lists three core competencies in the company that lead to creating customer value:

---

[*] From February 2014 Road Show presentation by Joe Raver, president and CEO, www.hillenbrand. com.

1. Strategy management: A focus on developing an effective game plan and execution of the critical few objectives that generate the best results.
2. Lean business: Lean business is the backbone of its cultural execution. It has proven even a slow growth industry can drive superior business results by employing continuous improvement and Lean business practices throughout the entire value chain, including acquisitions.
3. Intentional talent development: By managing leadership development of high-potential candidates through a variety of assignments, it is able to create a strong pipeline for succession planning. Mentoring and coaching has become a standard work process and expectation for management.

Hillenbrand thus has discovered the keys to Lean for the long term, a company cultural focus on continuous improvement, eliminating business waste, and developing people to be steeped in the Lean management system in the succession planning pipeline. It is deploying its focus on Lean to its acquisitions as part of bringing them on board.

To further establish and embed the importance of the Lean approach, the Hillenbrand board of directors has defined the job descriptions of all company officers in these two items:

1. Strengthen our corporate capabilities by ensuring that resources, processes, procedures, and controls necessary to be a successful, compliant, efficient, and well-controlled public company are in place. This will be accomplished through the application of the principles of Lean business across the enterprise.
2. Support the operating companies by providing necessary and sufficient resources to continue to generate profitable organic and acquisition growth that generates strong, predictable cash flows. This will be accomplished through a transparent resource allocation process and a commitment to a Lean organization and leadership talent development, at both the corporate and operating company levels.

It is evident to us that Lean is here to stay for the long term at Hillenbrand.

Autoliv

Autoliv is a Swedish American company that is most famous for its seat belts and airbag deployment systems in automobiles. Annual sales are $8.3 billion, and it has captured about 40% of the worldwide market with 80 facilities in

29 countries. In May 2014 it announced the appointment of a new chairman, Jan Carlson, who was the prior president and CEO from 2007 since joining AutoLiv in 1999, and has been deeply involved in Autoliv's Lean journey. Its Lean journey began in 2001–2002 and a Lean management system has been adopted. Since that time the stock price has risen from $40.06 per share January 1, 1999, to $102.97 as of May 21, 2014.

Another financial measure showing the results achieved by Autoliv is the 2013 productivity, revenue per employee: $191,134. In comparison, Delphi, a much larger automotive parts manufacturer, generated $16.463 billion in revenue in 2013 with 160,000 employees, for a productivity ratio of $103,893 per person. Autoliv was almost two times more productive.

In Table 6.1 the earnings per share (EPS) over this 5-year period, which included the 2008–2009 economic downturn, has increased from $2.29 to $5.09, or 222%! Return on capital has increased from 8.7 to 22.1%—a gain of 254%! Return on capital is in the upper range.

Additionally, the return on equity for ALV shows that it is able to reinvest its earnings as efficiently as its competitors in the auto and truck parts industry. Typically, companies that have higher return on equity values are more attractive to investors.

During that time Autoliv has aggressively created and adopted the Autoliv Production System (APS) to guide the company in its business strategy and culture. It states: "APS is the formalization of Autoliv's manufacturing culture sharing experiences and best practices." But more importantly, we also see a statement that it is focused on the entire company:

> The APS is the formalization of the Autoliv business culture based on the Toyota Production System to help every single Autoliv plant grow toward excellence.*

So, it agrees that the culture of the company is a business system, not just for manufacturing.

Table 6.1 Autoliv Key Financials

	2008	*2009*	*2010*	*2011*	*2012*	*2013*
EPS	2.29	$0.12	$6.77	$6.99	$5.17	$5.09
Return on capital	8.7%	2.2%	28.2%	27.5%	21.3%	22.1%

---

* www.autoliv.com, Products and Innovations Tab.

In addition, its performance, industry awards it has received, and its word of mouth reputation have grown enormously.

Based on the many requests for benchmarking visits, Autoliv created a new business unit that is charted to teach its approach to Lean to others. If there is anything the CEO likes, it is additional sales and revenue, so this is a definite positive addition to the company's portfolio! The APS is the way it does business, and during a plant tour, it is easy to witness many innovations in how it uses Lean tools and motivates the employees that are revolutionary. The employees, however, are oblivious to how APS is radically different from most American industry. It is just the way Autoliv does business, part of their training and daily standard work environment.

Quite a thing to see in person!

Toyota

As the inventor of the Toyota Production System, let's look at just a few of Toyota's financial achievements that are enviable by all and certainly are on Wall Street, upper management, and the CEO's minds:

- Profit was consistently been greater than that of Ford, GM, and Chrysler combined from 1994–2003.
- Profit every year over the last 48 years except 2009.
- Market cap (outstanding shares × share price) is greater than that of any other automobile company.

In addition, it operates the fastest automobile product development process in the world. Cars and trucks take less than 12 months to design compared to competitors, who typically take 2 to 3 years.

In Liker's book *The Toyota Way*, he summarizes: Toyota's "success is ultimately based on its ability to cultivate leadership, teams and culture to devise strategy, to build supplier relationships, and to maintain a learning organization."

This is a snapshot of how Toyota has woven continuous improvement and respect for people into its business system or, in our terminology, a Lean management system.

Lean Measures Turn into Financial Measures

As we've mentioned, the stock price is the most visible indication that the company is going in the right direction for investors, but in our viewpoint it is a short-term measure and is limited to many external influences, such as the economy, a sales announcement, new leadership coming in, old leadership leaving, market segment projections, company recalls, pending litigation, and investor emotions, among others. The CEO and upper management must navigate these short-term rough seas and need to have a stable company culture that can be aligned with common goals and is capable of recognizing and addressing both challenges and opportunities rapidly. While the revenue and earnings performance is usually at the top of investors' minds, it's important that the leadership understand the key balance sheet financial measures and the levers that can be exerted by resource application to drive value or return on invested capital. Here we need to address the balance sheet.

George Koenigsaecker clarifies for us the approach and explanations* of three key balance sheet financials and how they are directly keyed to Lean activities. Return on invested capital measures how efficiently company management is able to reinvest its earnings. These are some of the Lean levers that directly affect the financials scorecard of the CEO:

Working capital: By reducing cycle times and increasing inventory turns you can decrease the working capital required to run the business and have more cash for investment in new products.

Fixed capital: By reducing cycle times, you also increase flow and capacity. An advanced Lean company can run with one quarter of the capital equipment required by a normal company, as George states in his book.

Debt: By freeing up working capital and increasing your margins, you can pay down your debt at a much faster pace, thus allowing decisions to proceed rapidly on new investments!

Typically, companies that have higher return on invested capital value are more attractive to investors. These three balance sheet financials are strong contributors to every CEO's report card and feed directly to Wall Street investors' view of the company value, and hence stock price.

---

* George Koenigsaecker, *Leading the Lean Enterprise*, CRC Press, Boca Raton, FL, 2009.

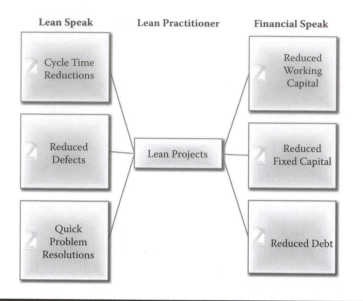

Figure 6.3 Converting Lean speak to financial speak.

In Figure 6.3 we see that these examples of converting Lean speak to financial speak have the Lean facilitator in the middle of the conversation, and he or she must be the translator to the CEO and upper management.

Management Questions about Continuous Improvement Projects

One of the first questions the CEO or other upper managers usually will ask is: How much will it cost and what is the payback? The focus should also be on another factor: Are you trying to improve revenue growth or profitability or both? On individual projects we must address these questions before there will be a real audience to hear the rest of the project plan. The CEO may feel good about the project and may already have an opinion, but he is looking at when does the financial improvement drop to the bottom line and what is the magnitude? Is it a one-time benefit, or will it be a continuing gold mine? We suggest the Lean practitioner have the facts and figures to quickly respond to these questions before the project discussion begins. Avoid as many unanswered questions as possible up front by having done the research and analysis first. Asking upper management to "trust me" or to envision the benefit puts a stranglehold on a positive go-ahead decision.

The first piece of data needed by upper management is to understand the proposed value creation in growth or profitability through cost savings or customer focus. Value can come from new products, new services, and effective operations and customer care. This will give upper management a feel for the magnitude of the value of the project; i.e., is it a small, medium, or large impact to the bottom line? It answers the real underlying question: "How excited should I be?"

In our example company introduced in Chapter 5, Amalgam, Inc., we mentioned that Amalgam leadership should look at financial impact, performance drivers, and organizational strategy to define actions and targets for change. The CEO will want to see the details—do not ask the CEO to "trust me."

So a definite tie to organizational strategy, financial value added, and performance drivers is needed. Let's discuss these in more detail, and in Chapter 7 we will dig into Amalgam's major issues to illustrate.

Organizational strategy is the driver of all change and priorities for the CEO and upper management, so the Lean practitioner must make a definite tie to the top priorities to gain understanding and support.

- Does it support growth and how?
- Does it support productivity and cost savings and how?
- What other strategies does the company support this year and how will this support those as well?

Addressing the financial element, the Lean practitioner needs to generate a good estimate of the implementation resources and the sustaining resources required, and a realistic schedule of the project timeline and implementation date is critical. Pretty easy for serious Lean practitioners accustomed to cost estimates—just calculate the cost of the value stream process in the current state and the realistic cost of the proposed future state with all the improvements cranked in, evaluating both labor and material. Also include internal stakeholders' input and how it will affect commitment and employee involvement. Most important changes have major effects on people and their work. Major categories to include are:

- Implementation resources required:
  Staffing: Lean practitioners, supervisors, direct workers.
  Support staffing: HR, support engineering, quality inspectors, process engineers, tooling engineers, quality engineers, IT staff, purchasing, etc.
  Investment: Software, tooling, travel, hardware, computers.

Estimated hours for each of these functions and the associated costs.
■ Sustaining resources:
Identify the current state sustaining resources—staffing and support labor in hours and dollars per month and per year
Compare to the future state sustaining resources for your projection of the cost savings on a monthly, yearly basis.
■ Scheduling estimates, which should include:
Time phased needs for the resources
Process times that are agreed to by each support group and function
Allowance for some problems and problem resolutions
A beta test to validate the approach
An implementation date when the new process will be online and checked out
■ Internal stakeholders' inputs:
Process owner's support and barriers
Disruption to flow
Jobs/people affected and consequences

For the performance drivers' element, the Lean practitioner will need to identify how to measure the success of the suggested change. The company will no doubt have some strategic metrics on quality, cost, customer satisfaction/delight, financial, and employees. How will the change affect them and will any conflict with each other?

How will the change affect the building blocks of Lean—continuous improvement and respect for people?

The Lean practitioner will need a 5-minute elevator speech covering the three elements and four financial topics, because that may be all the time allowed in the CEO's busy schedule.

William Baker's Experience

My personal experience with this approach comes from a meeting I had with the Raytheon business president of a $2 billion business operation. With the short face time I had with him, I was prepared for a detailed review of a continuous improvement project. What I found out was that he drilled down rapidly to the value created, the resources required, and the timeframe of implementing the changes. He was also interested to know if the stakeholders and process owners had agreed to the possible impact and changes and how we would measure success. I actually had about 10 minutes to address his concerns, and then he was ready to move onto the next topic. What I learned was that he expected what we used to call in the U.S. Air Force "completed staff work." The Air Force standard work description of this approach was to do the research and address all the implementation problems and concerns, so the commander could ask questions and then sign the orders with potential problems already researched and resolutions mapped out.

Of course, the backup plan is the 30-minute detailed overview to demonstrate the depth and breadth of your research, including the projected value over time.

After all the data collection and analysis has been done, the Lean practitioner will have a good grasp of company strategy, project scope, costs, and timeframe to be able to clearly communicate to upper management and gain project acceptance. However, if the use of resources is too high or conflicts with other priorities, this can affect project go-ahead. The Lean practitioner may not be aware of the other priorities or the resources already assigned, but with a good, clear, concise project proposal and value added, the worst result can be a rescheduling and postponement. Depending on the company focus, if it happens to be profit recovery, for example, the Lean practitioner can cover the benefits to working capital, fixed capital, and debt, as well as immediate cost savings and long-term cost savings, to convince the CEO he has a real effective Lean strategy to implement his company strategy. If the focus is on revenue growth, some of the same investment benefits need to apply to the sales process, new products, and expected revenue impact. The Lean practitioner will enhance the standing of Lean, himself, and his ability to help the CEO generate company value for all stakeholders.

Helping Upper Management Achieve Lean for the Long Term

The Lean practitioner can help the CEO and upper management by being intimately knowledgeable of the company's business model using the strategic framework as shown in Chapter 4 (Figure 4.6a), to illustrate the company connection of Lean continuous improvement tactics. As a practitioner you may not be asked to help, but you need to be ready as needed, when the opportunity arises. This knowledge and your persuasion ability can help add to your own personal value within the organization, if you know what is needed to achieve excellence. Some of the key questions that you need to be aware of follow in our discussion.

Company Strategy

Does our company strategy define Lean as a building block to our future success? Does everyone understand Lean is our way of doing business, both short term and long term? For example, refer to the Danaher Business System (DBS) as a best practice and the references on its website (www.danaher.com) and its conference presentations that state that the DBS is its competitive advantage. This was an ingredient that was missing from the Company X example in Chapter 2. Lean was an operations thing and missing from the leadership team, administrative, and sales and marketing functions.

- What performance drivers will generate changes in the needed focus areas?
- Does any change require board approval or a board briefing?

Mentoring People

What are the expectations placed on leadership that drive their behavior by taking appropriate risks and mentoring others—leadership meetings, Gemba walks, customer talks, and encouraging others to continually make changes to improve?

When Texas Instruments began the journey, the leadership team rarely met face-to-face, since the businesses were separated widely by location, geography, technology, and customers and were not close to the fabrication manufacturing sites. It made sense at the time. But when the new president came in with a focus on continuous improvement and respect for people, he began to hold leadership team meetings every Monday morning and assigned each vice president specific areas of accountability where they had to work across businesses and functions. This relatively simple change had a big change on culture and how they did things. The leadership team began to work with each other since the president expected problems to be addressed outside the team meetings and no longer could anyone come in and point fingers; they were expected to have solutions to problems. They actually began to mentor each other and share knowledge! This set a new tone on mentoring and working together. It forces the following questions:

- How often do we talk to each other at the management level?
- What effects will any planned changes have on our people; have they had their input?
- Are the stakeholders and process owners on board?
- Does everyone have a mentor?
- Who are you mentoring?

Customers

What are the current and future needs (both stated and unstated) of our current customers? Will new technologies change their expectations and needs?

How can we best serve them so they are delighted rather than satisfied? Delighted customers return for subsequent sales; satisfied ones may not. Some significant technological shifts made new industry leaders and relegated old standards to distant, small market players. Consider Kodak, as we mentioned in Chapter 4, the once proud and mighty leader in photos via film technology and photos, and then came the evolution to digital photo technology applications like Instagram, Facebook, Shutterfly, and smart phones with camera capability. Kodak sat on its hands while the new technology and customer needs passed it by, and it did not have a business model that looked to changing times and moving away from the old technology and creating new markets. It was trying to hang on to market leadership in old technology, but the world passed it by.

The same can be said of Sony, who was the undisputed leader in early mobile musical technology via radios and the Walkman product lines, but with the next step in technology, Apple leapfrogged it to iPads, iPhones, and iTunes, which became the new industry standard expectation. Change continues as Sony is staging a comeback in high-technology cameras, in 2014, by adding new technology and features not offered by old-time standard brands like Canon and Nikon. So some companies can learn and move on, as long as they recognize their burning platform in time. Fuji is facing the same technology and markets, but restructured to create a new business model.

The customers may not know what they need just yet, but they do know they want convenience and access at a reasonable cost. Technology shifts generate very specific questions, but only the transforming companies survive, and the questions need to be asked:

Growth

- How will changes affect our planned growth?
- Will they accelerate our plans and require replanning of people, facilities, and cash flow?
- What other unintended consequences and effects can we anticipate?

Financial

- What is the revenue impact?
- Do we have a value stream map that accurately captures the current state?
- What steps are non-value added and can be deleted?
- What resources will it take to make changes, and what effects will there be on our stakeholders?
- What are the projected savings?

Suppliers

- How will changes affect our supply chain partners?
- Can we include them in our approach and have them help us design the implementation?
- Can they respond to support our new plan?
- How can we partner with our suppliers for the long term vs. being on separate sides?

Culture

- What behavior drivers need to be in place to generate a real team/people-based company?
- Does the culture support rapid learning cycles, although it may not be perfect?

A quick summary is shown in Figure 6.4, used since 2007. It addresses some important aspects of how a Lean management system can become embedded in the company, and once embedded, a snapshot of what Lean management looks like to the employees and outsiders.

Lean Management System

How to embed Lean Management in the overall Business Management System

Successful lean companies embed lean in the business management system by:

➢ Creating an overall lean business strategy taught by the leaders

➢ Defining continuous improvement as "how we do business"

➢ Cultivating a respect for people philosophy by coaching and mentoring at all levels

What a Lean company with Lean management looks like
- Lean is part of the company vision and mission
- Lean is for all departments, business units and upper management
- The Board knows that Lean is "the" company culture, believes in lean and grows management from within
- Lean starts with the customer, is based on the respect for people and continuously and aggressively looks for better ways to do things at all levels

Figure 6.4   Lean management system.

The Indianapolis race car depicts the speed required in our transformations and the competitive nature of the race to excellence.[*]

---

[*] From a Speed To Excellence presentation first presented by Bill Baker in 2007.

Chapter 7

As a Lean Practitioner, What Your CEO Wants You to Know

Introduction

In Chapter 6 we highlighted how the Hillenbrand board of directors has defined the job descriptions of all company officers in these two items:

1. Strengthen our corporate capabilities by ensuring that resources, processes, procedures, and controls necessary to be a successful, compliant, efficient, and well-controlled public company are in place. This will be accomplished through the application of the principles of Lean Business across the enterprise.
2. Support the operating companies by providing necessary and sufficient resources to continue to generate profitable organic and acquisition growth that generates strong, predictable cash flows. This will be accomplished through a transparent resource allocation process and a commitment to a Lean organization and leadership talent development, at both the corporate and operating company levels.

While we see today many companies claim to be doing Lean, unfortunately what we find is there are few companies that have created the kind of clarity that Hillenbrand has expressed. What is all too common is that many senior managers perceive Lean as tactical and not strategic. Lean is for manufacturing, and manufacturing examples do not apply easily into business processes. Lean training programs emphasize tools, with little emphasis on desired cultural changes. When Lean successes occur, they are not widely communicated, and those that are publicized are seen with suspicion. Managers at companies with Lean programs think of it as an expense and not an investment. People are sent to training and sites appoint a Lean specialist to satisfy a corporate requirement. Managers continue to be held accountable for results, not the means to achieve results, so most delegate Lean leadership somewhere down in the organization. A recent general manager's comment captures the widespread sentiment: "I won't get fired for not doing Lean; I will get fired for missing a delivery." So what we find is Lean practitioners are spending their time in limited areas of the company and, as a result, do not have the impact on company performance that management would like to see or gets their attention.

Let's refer to Amalgam, Inc.'s cost structure in Figure 7.1 to consider where most of the Lean literature and examples are focused. What we see is that the majority of Lean efforts are focused on a small fraction of the total cost of doing business. In Amalgam's case it is less than a quarter of the cost structure. It's hard to make a significant impact when 75% of the cost structure is off the table.

Unless the company is directing its attention to the total cost structure, Lean efforts are having little impact on company performance. This should be no surprise, as direct labor in production and warehousing has become

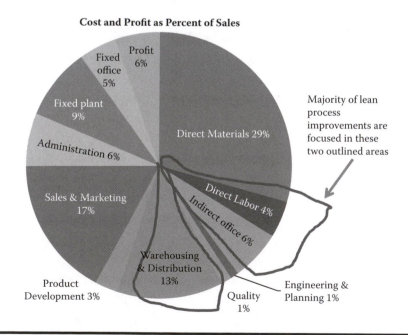

Figure 7.1   Cost and profit as percent of sales.

a smaller and smaller part of overall total costs. This is due to a multitude of factors, including improvements made with Lean methodologies.

In recent years we have seen manufacturing in the United States starting to make a comeback. Driven by increasing costs of complex and lengthy supply chains, energy costs, and more competitive labor, companies are increasing U.S. factory jobs and moving to produce products closer to their customers. The surge in oil and natural gas production has pushed down energy costs in the United States, and wages in China and some other emerging countries have reduced their overall wage advantage. The Boston Consulting Group publication "Made in America Again"[*] concludes that the total cost of production, shipping, and other costs for many products make it more economical to make some products in the United States than in Asia.

Simplifying sourcing location analysis for individual companies, Harry C. Moser, founder and president of the Reshoring Initiative, created a total cost comparison tool: The Total Cost of Ownership Estimator. The model enables companies to aggregate all the costs and risks factors of offshore sourcing into one cost for simpler decision making. Many times the analysis indicates the rising wages in China and other logistics costs have negated the cost advantage previously seen as justification for outsourcing to China. The estimator tool is available for free in the Reshoring Initiative website, www.reshorenow.org.

Costs, however, are not the only consideration, since energy costs have become less a factor as companies have reduced usage over the years. These days, companies are increasingly focused on building to demand and reacting quickly to changes in customers' needs and preferences. Being nimble reduces the risk that companies will miss market shifts and be stuck with excess stocks of unsalable items or a shortage of items they could sell.

In spite of this, lots of well-intentioned, hard-working people spend a ton of hours compiling best practices, developing content, and performing assessments only to see a distinct lack of real impact in the business unit or the company. This needs to change. Lean practitioners need to move beyond the typical process activities in their Lean activities and look holistically at the business performance and imperatives. It is well known that 80% of the cost of product materials and direct labor is determined in product development before the first product is produced, for example. Additionally, referring to Figure 7.1, we see in Amalgam, Inc.'s cost structure that the sum of sales and marketing, administration, and fixed costs exceeds the cost impact of materials.

---

[*] Harold L. Sirkin, Michael Zinger and Douglas Hohner, *Made in America Again*, Boston, Consulting Group, 2011.

Many companies have set up Lean staffs and promotion departments, and while there are differences in each company, the work tends to be similar, including but not limited to:

- Defining a common set of best practices and work standards
- Assessing the maturity profile of the plants against these best practices and standard work
- Helping to plan and facilitate improvement events
- Providing instructional content, tools and templates, and other materials to assist sites in implementing the best practices locally

It would be hard to argue that the work described above isn't important. It seems clear that a company serious about driving consistent improvement to its business needs to establish a common set of practices and standards. Toyota, Danaher, and other high-performing Lean companies label their management systems (TPS and DBS, for example) and strive for consistency in developing their people.

The missing element in many of the Lean promotion offices is a clear connection with the company's business model and priorities with a holistic view. Too often their sandbox is too small to make a large impact. Consequently, they concentrate on tools, techniques, and auditing "Lean maturity" in operations, missing R&D, sales and marketing, administration, HR, and finance, whose departments seem to have the gift of skipping the whole Lean experience, thinking it to be irrelevant to them. The perspective is therefore too focused on details and not on the business model.

A business model describes the rationale of how an organization creates, delivers, and captures value, in economic, social, cultural, or other contexts. The process of business model construction is usually a part of business strategy development and review. Business models are used to describe and classify businesses, especially in entrepreneurial settings, as readers of *Inc.*, *Fast Company*, and other such magazines might recognize. They are also used by managers inside companies to clarify strategies, diagnose business problems, and explore possibilities for future development. The essence of a business model is illustrated in Figure 7.2.

Consider the findings in Amalgam, Inc. in Chapter 5. (Remember: We are using Amalgam as our illustration. It is a company that is a combination of cases from real companies, but not all in the same company, as presented here.) Amalgam had acquired multiple companies and locations as well as added hundreds of product lines to its product portfolio. What Amalgam

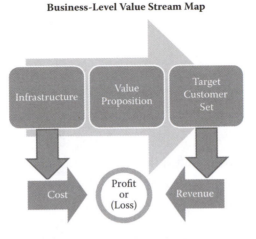

Figure 7.2 Business-level value stream map.

found is that a large portion of the products are unprofitable, which combined with a complex infrastructure has put service delivery, customer service, and quality level below par for its industry. The business situation has presented the CEO and his senior management team with multidimensional issues. It might be understandable that they would not have a great deal of interest in Lean if they do not see how it would contribute to solutions to their problems.

So how would a Lean practitioner look at the situation at Amalgam, Inc.? To answer the question, we simply need to fall back on the fundamental principles of Lean, which start from the customer and the value customers require. Consider, for example, constructing business-level value stream maps of the current and future states and what is required to support the business:

1. Identify the customers your business is targeting.
2. Describe the value customers are expecting and define the demand (volume).
3. Scope the required infrastructure to support the segment identified, which includes the products or services, distribution footprint (such as local stocking or remote, make to order or ship from stock, standard or custom product, etc.), and the processes required to deliver the value.
4. In the future state map, describe how the new infrastructure is different from what exists today. What is required for the new model, including labor, overhead, and capital?

In the mapping process we will need to analyze the business model and infrastructure currently in the company and the future to determine if there are any significant differences that require us to take action. We will now go to Amalgam, Inc. to illustrate the four steps we noted above. The issues we found in Amalgam, Inc. in Chapter 5 are declining margins and customer service as a result of:

1. The multiple locations, which created complex and redundant management structures, adding millions in cost, as well as creating competing demand for capital, operations, sales, and R&D resources.
2. A counterproductive proliferation of products that did not create demand, but cannibalized each other, thereby reducing the economies of scale for materials and manufacturing.

   While the temptation is to focus on the cost structure first, Lean principles suggest we start with the customer.

Identify the Customer Segments and Their Characteristics

First a note: We do not expect everyone to be a marketing expert in this analysis, but to suggest the Lean practitioner use his or her skills in leading cross-functional teams to bring marketing into the analysis. Marketing managers frequently use common segmentation differentiators, which include geographic, demographic, psychographic, and behavioristic characteristics, to identify and define target markets.

Segmentation Characteristics

1. **Geographics:** The location, size of the area, density, and climate zone of your customers.
2. **Demographics:** The age, gender, income, family composition and size, occupation, and education of your customers.
3. **Psychographics:** The general personality, behavior, lifestyle, rate of use, repetition of need, benefits sought, and loyalty characteristics of your customers.
4. **Behaviors:** The needs they seek to fulfill, the level of knowledge, information sources, and attitude, use, or response to a product by your customers.

Customer or market segmentation is simply the grouping together of customers based on similarities they share with respect to any dimensions relevant to your business that allows the business to better satisfy customers' needs. Dimensions could include customer needs, channel preferences, interest in specific product features, customer profitability, etc. The customers should be grouped into segments by like characteristics to make this meaningful. The best segmentation is one that is similar as a group and distinctly different from other segments.

The important task is to determine how to segment (or group) your customers in a way that will have the biggest impact on your business. The best way to address this is to define the objective for the segmentation in the first place. In other words, you must first define what you want the segmentation to do for your business. Typical segment objectives are to:

- Develop new products
- Create segmented ads and marketing communications
- Develop differentiated customer servicing and retention strategies
- Target prospects with the greatest profit potential
- Optimize sales channel mix

In Amalgam, Inc. we find customers at two ends of the spectrum of the product line analysis: the high-volume runners with broad customer activity and the low-volume items with few customers. The graphs in Figure 7.3 illustrate the disproportionate distribution of customer activity, revenue, and profitability of the products. Approximately 40% of the product lines provide most of the revenue, profit, and customer activity for Amalgam, Inc. We also see a large number of product lines have little activity and profit and, as we find later in our analysis, consume resources and rob profit.

Customer Value and Demand

Customer value is the benefit that a customer will get from a product or service in comparison with its cost. This benefit might be measured in monetary terms, such as when a product helps save the customer money that can then be spent on something else. Some benefits can be difficult to quantify, such as the utility or enjoyment that a customer receives from a product or service. It refers to the value that the customers receive, not to how valuable customers are. The term *customer value* should not be confused

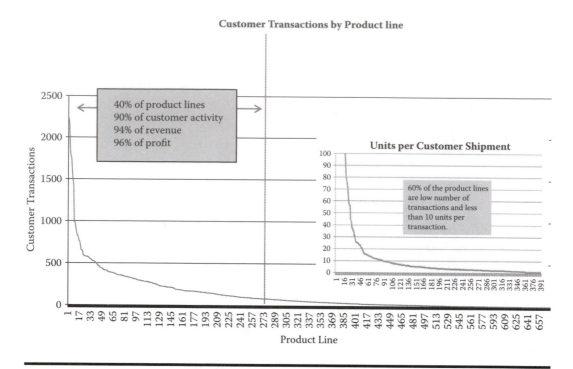

Figure 7.3 Customer transactions by product line.

with the value of customers to the business, which is the other side of the consideration.

As Lean practitioners, we are trained to look at customer value and what you do as a company to deliver that value. Lean is customer-centric, so value must be examined from the point of view of the customer. In segmenting the customers, we are grouping them by similar characteristics. Some customer segments value certain products or attributes more than others. Some segments may have very unique and specific requirements. The key is to optimize products and services for specific segments to distinguish the business to its target customers. Communicating that the business has made the choice to distinguish itself in that way in the organization is important to align the organization with the business strategy.

While Peter Drucker noted that the first order of business is to find a customer, the central idea behind finding a customer is that the business will create something of value to one or more customers who, in turn, are willing to pay enough to make the venture worthwhile. When we look at Amalgam's product lines in Figure 7.4, we are looking at the customer activity. In this case, the customers have identified their preference for products by their behavior in terms of purchasing practices regarding the products

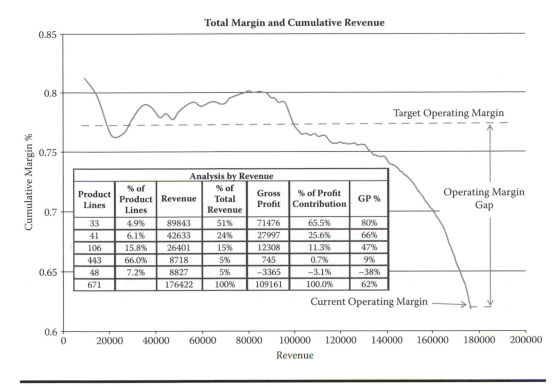

Figure 7.4   Total margin and cumulative revenue.

they are buying. In the next level of analysis we can look at revenues and margins and who is buying the products and their behavior in terms of purchasing practice; we can do a simplified analysis by grouping the products as done in Figure 7.4 to create an estimate of the potential for improvement.

However, margins are typically calculated from standard product cost, which can be misleading. In Amalgam's situation, the standard cost analysis initially indicated all products to be profitable. This was due to the standard allocation of overhead to products and not considering SG&A (Selling, General, & Administrative Expenses) in the analysis.

The product lines for the customers that represent the tail in Figure 7.3 contribute a significant profit gap. In this analysis the customers were grouped by buying behavior patterns, and the infrastructure support in sales, customer service, marketing, distribution, and manufacturing was allocated based on the cost of an order. This changed the peanut butter standard cost approach to somewhat of an activity-based cost system without all the precision and effort of activity-based costing. We use the adjusted standard cost to illustrate how products contribute to the revenues and profitability of the business without getting bogged down in detailed analysis. If we are 80% in the right ballpark, we can use the information to guide our efforts and estimate the business impact. We see in Figure 7.4 that Amalgam has considerable improvement opportunity, as indicated by the operating margin gap, which totals around $20 million.

Scope the Required Infrastructure

Lean practitioners can use the business unit value stream mapping and analysis (VSM&A) tool in this step of the analysis. The purpose of a business or business unit VSM is to create a focused visual of the business models (more detailed than Figure 7.2) that serves as a way to describe the current and desired future business models. It describes the required infrastructure to support the segment identified, which includes the products and services, distribution footprint (such as local stocking or remote, make to order or ship from stock, standard or custom product, etc.), and the actions required to move from the current to the future state. The intent of value stream assessment is to take a macro look at the business in a compressed time-frame with an eye for identifying opportunities for performance improvements across the breadth of the enterprise.

The key to success of the VSM&A event is to clearly define the scope of the analysis to be done. Specifically, what is in scope and what is out of scope is important. Businesses can be described in terms of value streams, and all businesses have four fundamental value streams, as illustrated Figure 7.5.

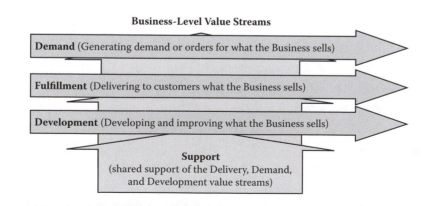

Business-Level Value Streams

Demand (Generating demand or orders for what the Business sells)

Fulfillment (Delivering to customers what the Business sells)

Development (Developing and improving what the Business sells)

Support
(shared support of the Delivery, Demand, and Development value streams)

Figure 7.5   Business-level value streams.

Example Value Stream Identification Table.

Value Stream Definition Matrix		Customer or Market			
		Commercial		Government	
		Major account	Small accounts	Aero space	Other
Product or Service	Simple recurring		X		
	Complex recurring	X	X		
	Small lot prototype			X	
	Pushing state of the art			X	X

Figure 7.6 Example value stream identification table.

Describing the business in this manner provides a language for communicating within the company as well as among supply chain partners that share common processes.

The first step is to define the broad scope of the value streams to be analyzed. It could be the total business level or one of the four value streams. This depends on the business needs.

The second level of scoping is to define the number of value streams included in the selected level. The tool we use to make this selection is the product and customer matrix shown in Figure 7.6.

The matrix columns are customer types and are subsegmented, and the rows are the major product or service types. Each X represents a possible value stream. Note that some value streams are not unique, so group them together if they share planning systems, or logistics networks, or manufacturing processes, or are managed together. Do not group them if they are distinct types such as build to order vs. build to stock, or have unique geographies, or unique manufacturing processes. Each group is considered a logical value stream for further work.

When planning the value stream activity, the scope of the effort can be described using the above general value streams to create a common focus. This is built into the charter for the VSM&A event to allow the team in the event process to analyze the value stream at the appropriate level of detail and establishes the basis of the competitive performance targets to be set.

Improvement targets for the VSM&A events need to be breakthrough-level performance shifts. Targets such as achieving market-winning fulfillment time with the least inventory risk in a make-to-order business environment or achieving lowest total cost to customer solutions are common goals.

Business-Level Metrics

	Attribute	Metric (Business Level)
Customer	Reliability	Perfect order fulfillment
	Responsiveness	Order fulfillment cycle time
	Flexibility	Supply chain flexibility
		Supply chain adaptability
Internal	Cost	Supply chain management cost
		Cost of goods sold
	Assets	Cash to cash cycle time
		Return on fixed assets
		Return on working capital

Figure 7.7   Metrics table.

Selecting the right goals for the business is important in the preparation for the event. In the case of our company, Amalgam, Inc., we are looking to define the infrastructure required to eliminate the cost performance gap while improving customer service.

Value stream maps are focused on work processes in the value stream and can be described and measured with process metrics. Those metrics need to be both internal and external. Standard metrics for a business-level VSM&A are shown in Figure 7.7.

Performance improvement needs are set in concert with the strategic direction of the company and the competitive marketplace. The metrics then are evaluated to determine where the business needs to perform superior to the competition, at above average, or simply at parity with the rest of the competitors. Each unique combination of ratings defines your value stream strategy for the channel.

Rate the metrics in three levels of business requirements:

1. Superior: Be in the top 10% of the competitive market. The business must be superior in this performance parameter to take market share. Generally, do not have more than one attribute identified as superior.
2. Above average: Be in the top 50% of the competitive market to maintain or gain business.
3. Parity: We need parity to be in the business, but it's not a differentiator for any company.

Value Stream Strategy Matrix

	Performance Attribute	Competitive requirements			
		Value stream 1	Value stream 2	Value stream 3	Value stream 4
Customer Facing	Reliability				
	Responsiveness				
	Flexibility				
Internal Facing	Cost				
	Assets				

Figure 7.8   Value stream strategy matrix.

Evaluate customer facing as well as internal attributes. Using a matrix such as that shown in Figure 7.8 is helpful to create focus for the analysis.

Describe the Future State and Actions to Get There

The objective of the mapping exercise is not to drive down to the infinite detail, but to scope out a picture to describe how the future state is different from what exists today. Its purpose is to identify a well-grounded set of aspirations to the size of the opportunity that warrants the topic on the CEO's agenda. What would that mean from a product offering and business model infrastructure, including labor, overhead, and capital? In the case of Amalgam, we would want to know how many product lines remain and the impact on profitability of the company, as well as revenue. We illustrate this in the current and future state fulfillment process maps in Figure 7.9.

The fact that Amalgam has become a very complex business in products and locations through its acquisitive growth strategy suggests we cannot simply focus on the number of product lines. While this is an important component of improving service and profitability, it is only half of the answer. Reducing the number of sites that add disproportionately large costs to Amalgam's business is required as well. This leads the VSM effort to a two-pronged strategy: improve the ability to service target customers and reduce the number of unprofitable products overall.

Providing a clearer picture of the site redundancy and number of functional departments, the current organizations required totals 160.

Current and Future State Maps
(Fulfillment Value Stream)

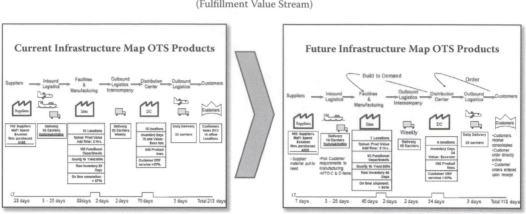

Figure 7.9   Current and future state maps.

Results

Given the holistic picture, the value stream map constructed, including the product line analysis and site redundancy, it became easier to see and make broad-based changes (transformations), starting with eliminating unprofitable products and then reducing the overall asset footprint of the company's operations. Taking these actions put the company in a position to improve plant and distribution center loading while improving to a competitive service level and lead time. Amalgam's projects are a consolidation of separate companies, and the list of results below are also consolidated from separate companies but are real outcomes. They are listed here to illustrate the magnitude of improvement when a Lean Management System is adopted across a total company. Some of what can be expected from adopting a lean management system and the tenacity to drive continuous improvement across the entire business organization including business acquisitions is illustrated below:

- Above industry peer revenue growth
- The product lines trimmed by 45% while growing the business and profits.
- Inventories reduced by 45%.
- The product stocking portfolio thinned by 60%.
- Service level and lead time improved by 10 points and 55%, respectively.

- Distribution locations consolidated for 50% reduction while improving service.
- The manufacturing footprint reduced from 15 sites to 7 balancing capacity to demand.
- Functional departments reduced by 40%.
- Increased funding from operating cash flow for R&D by 100% contributing to significant organic growth.

The changes improved Amalgam, Inc.'s income statement and growth performance, allowing the company to strengthen its sales and marketing while keeping the general and administrative costs relatively flat. In Figure 7.10, we show the functions and their organization across all the geographical locations in North America, Europe and Asia that aided in VSM analysis and provided broad strategy deployment. After 5 years, operating under the new structure, revenues grew by almost 70% and operating income by 300%. See Figure 7.11. Note the numbers have been adjusted, but represent real results. We used percentage relationships to make the numbers work to illustrate the point.

This type of major transformation moves the needle and puts companies in a position to benefit from their continuous improvement efforts. Improved income and cash generation provide the fuel to allow the company to invest in R&D, add acquisitions, and grow. However, transformations are difficult. Consider our example of National Cash Register and the NCR timeline in Chapter 5. The company, beginning in 1884, was the leader in mechanical cash registers for many years. In the 1960s that all began to change, and in the early 1970s the company had to make a gut-wrenching transition to electronic point of sale that had a major impact on the company organization. Later it was acquired by AT&T, and then again reemerged as an independent company, now marketing itself as a leader in consumer transaction technologies. Along the way it changed its name, its products, its asset footprint, its ownership, and its organization in order to survive.

Survival, as a business entity, is clearly not a given, as we have seen 87% of the original S&P 500 companies are not on the list today. Consider also Toyota, our model for Lean and continuous improvement. Toyota started as a small rural Japanese company and built itself into a large Japanese company, transforming itself into a global business, expanding to the luxury market, manufacturing and sourcing in market, and developing products that lead the auto industry. Toyota is also a model of continuous transformation.

The fear of impacting revenue is always a major reason that companies fail to act decisively on products, complex operational supply chains, and

Current Functional Matrix

Department/Function	Na Locations							Europe Locations									Asia Locations					Count
	Cal 1	Cal 2	Loc 3	East 1	East 2	Mid 1	North 1	Ger 1	Irl 2	Irl 1	Fr 2	Fr 1	Net 2	Isl 2	UK 1	Fr 3	Aus 1	Chn 2	Chn 3			
Corporate	X							X						X				X	X			5
Operations																						
Engineering/Sourcing		X				X					X	X	X									5
Quality	X	X	X	X	X	X		X		X	X	X	X	X				X				13
Purchasing/Planning	X	X	X	X	X	X		X		X		X	X									10
Manufacturing	X	X	X	X	X	X	X	X	X	X	X	X	X	X			X					15
Distribution	X	X	X	X	X			X		X		X	X				X					10
Product Refurbishment	X	X				X		X						X			X					6
Operation Reporting		X						X														2
																						0
Finance/Accounting																						
Information Technology	X	X	X	X	X			X		X		X	X	X			X	X	X			13
																						0
Financial Analysis	X							X		X		X										4
Financial Reporting	X							X		X		X	X		X							6
Accounts Payable	X							X		X		X	X		X							6
Accounts Receivable/Collections	X							X		X		X	X		X							6
Manufacturing Cost Accounting	X							X		X		X	X		X							6
Legal																						
Regulatory	X													X								2
Compliance	X													X								2
Human Resources	X	X	X		X			X		X		X	X	X	X							10
Sales/Marketing																						
Customer Service	X	X	X	X	X			X		X		X			X		X	X	X			12
Research & Development		X						X		X		X		X								5
Clinic WORKSHOP				X									X			X						3
Marketing	X	X						X		X		X	X	X				X	X			9
Sales	X	X		X				X		X		X	X	X				X	X			10
Count:	18	13	7	8	9	5	1	17	2	16	3	13	18	9	9	1	4	8	8	0	0	160

Figure 7.10 Current functional matrix.

Income Statement Changes

	Prior Year	Current	After Change	5 years later
Total Revenue	250000	257500	251750	435000
COGS	95314	100425	90630	165000
Gross Profit	154686	157075	161120	270000
Operating Expenses				
R & D	7500	6695	10070	22000
SG & A	124250	131325	120840	188000
Depreciation	7500	7725	7553	15250
Operating Income	15436	11330	22658	44750

Figure 7.11 Amalgam's income comparison.

sales and marketing strategies. But what we see at Amalgam, Inc. should not be a surprise. When these issues are addressed, we generally see revenues grow. The reason is that marginal products and location growth consume precious resources in disproportional amounts, confuse customers, and create process and organizational waste, all the while delivering subpar results. As the old saying has it, "Sales is vanity, profits is sanity, cash is reality." We would add, "Transformation is survival." After all, extinction is an option!

Takeaways

1. Breakdown the company cost and profit structure into a pie chart similar to Figure 7.1. How many of the departments of the total pie have lean practices that have been effective?

2. Identify the defined business segments in which the company operates. Can you diagram the unique business models that the company operates to create value in each segment? If so, do this on one page which illustrates the customer segment characteristics, the value proposition and the infrastructure required to deliver on the value proposition.

3. Does your company have future state(s) defined and roadmap(s) to get there?

4. Have you defined the gap between the future or ideal operating margin and current? How big is the opportunity?

Chapter 8

Lean across the Organization

A terrible tragedy occurred when just in time and lean thinking became known as lean manufacturing.

—Art Byrne, AME spring conference, San Antonio, 2013, keynote presentation

Art Byrne, former CEO of Wiremold Company and author of *The Lean Turnaround*, tells us that Lean is a business strategy, not simply a collection of manufacturing tools from which companies can pick and choose. He further goes on to say that companies that opt to adopt a Lean operating system as a company strategy will have a competitive advantage and will ultimately see better performance results than companies that simply implement a few Lean tools.

Lean can be a bit of a Rorschach test. We can all spell it, we all might define it somewhat differently, and companies have put their own brand on their business system. Toyota, of course, is well known for its Toyota Production System (TPS), which defines its business operating system. Toyota is also committed to managing for results and continuously improving the means to deliver those results. The phrase *business operating system* refers to a standard, enterprise-wide collection of business processes used in many companies and includes the common structure, principles, and practices necessary to drive the organization.

Diversified companies like Danaher, Autoliv, Hillenbrand, Honeywell, Illinois Tool Works, HNI, Pentair, and others we have discussed have adopted a standard, common collection of business processes or business process improvement methodologies.

- Danaher is well known for its Danaher Business System (DBS).
- Honeywell has established the Honeywell Operating System (HOS).
- Illinois Tool Works has its ITW Business Model.
- HNI operates in a member-owner and rapid continuous improvement environment.
- Pentair has developed its Pentair Integrated Management System (PIMS).
- Autoliv has its APS that drives its worldwide business.
- Hillenbrand has taken its business model to drive its acquisition and growth plans.

While the business operating systems may have different names at each company, they refer to the way the company manages complex business processes in a common way across its diverse portfolio of businesses. Taking a top-down view, each includes three key attributes:

1. Growth
2. Operational excellence
3. Leadership

What is distinctive about these business systems is that each company claims that it is their true competitive advantage. It is not uncommon for companies to publish vision, mission, and core values; however, for Lean companies it becomes who they are, their value set, and their culture. Some people think of that as a soft side, but it's probably the most important part. The hard side is what we see in plant tours through their facilities and is the application of the tools, techniques, and processes.

What is not so visible is how the management runs their operating companies on a day-to-day basis. It is not just about process efficiency, but what is done to drive growth and how they nurture and develop company leaders. Most importantly, however, is how all three of those efforts—growth, operational excellence, and leadership—are woven together to create a distinctive business operating system that extends across the entire organization, as depicted in Figure 8.1.

We will immerse ourselves again in Amalgam, Inc. to illustrate this as a Lean management system in action.

We will explore how Lean looks in the operating system fundamentals, and how it impacts the company performance with examples by referring again to the core management model as shown in Figure 8.2. We will talk about the soft side, the culture that is supported by the Lean management

Lean Business System Fundamentals

Intersecting area is where competitive advantage develops

Figure 8.1   Lean business system fundamentals.

model that we introduced in Chapter 2. The five key elements define for us what's important, what we expect of leaders, and leadership teams. Jim Collins counseled us in his book, *Good to Great*, to get the right people on the bus first and worry about where the bus goes second. We know that there is a premium on talent, but the best team wins when talent plays well together, i.e., teamwork. They know where they are going, what to expect from each other, can clearly see their progress, accept responsibility for the overall business goals, and are constantly working to do better. These are the essential elements of a Lean management system.

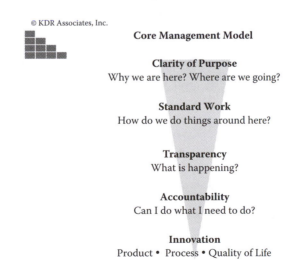

© KDR Associates, Inc.

Core Management Model

Clarity of Purpose
Why we are here? Where are we going?

Standard Work
How do we do things around here?

Transparency
What is happening?

Accountability
Can I do what I need to do?

Innovation
Product • Process • Quality of Life

Figure 8.2   Core management model.

While most of us are accustomed to examples from the production floor, Amalgam has opportunities for improvement across the organization, starting with its strategic business model. Using the core management model as a guide, we see some of the tools that apply in each element.

Strategically, we see Lean is really about growth, leadership, and process. Those are the three things that operating business leaders use to help build value and long-term success. They're all equally important.

There are some fundamental tools that are part of the Lean toolkit that support the management model, and they apply equally across every business segment and even across the major functions within a business. Figure 8.3 has identified some of the fundamental tools. We put the voice of the customer at both the top and the bottom of the tool list to illustrate the customer-centric nature of a Lean strategy.

Lean is customer-centric; when customers talk, we need to listen. The customer is the most important relationship a business has and it is the people of the company that nurture that relationship. A business cannot help itself, cannot grow unless its people are taking very good care of its customers. Sometimes that customer may be an internal customer; it may be the next person in the production line, the next department, or maybe a service rep somewhere in the world at a customer site needing support. The principal tenet of Lean is that it all starts with the customer.

Standard work is a term that we hear a lot, often thought about at workstations on the factory floor, but it applies equally within administrative and leadership processes as well. It's about defining consistent work processes for people to know what to expect from each other. It is also about achieving the desired quality of outcome through defined work processes, the

Management System Element	Focus	Some Tools
Clarity of Purpose	Alignment	Voice of Customer, Value Stream Mapping Strategic Framework
Standard Work	Quality	Standard work, Kaizen, Problem Solving, 5S
Transparency	Communications	Visual Management, Future State Map, Gemba walks
Accountability	Execution	Daily Management, Functional Plans, Kaizen
Innovation	Breakthrough	Voice of the Customer, 10 types of innovation, 3P

Figure 8.3   Lean management system support.

basis for holding each other accountable for achieving planned results, and also a baseline for continuous improvement across businesses.

Many of us have visited benchmark facilities and recognize 5S as about clean, safe, orderly work environments. 5S also provides the foundation for continuous improvement across businesses. Visual management, value stream mapping, and daily management practices that are open and transparent to every business associate help drive results across the businesses. So we encourage consistent application across businesses. As we have seen in Toyota, the tools are not executed exactly the same in every location, but in a very similar and consistent way regardless of the business, regardless of the region, to help drive results.

Innovation defines the future. Kaizen in a Lean company culture is a way of life, and there is a mindset that no matter how well a company does, it can always do better. That fuels intensity, a level of expectation, and a pace that drives change. Kaizen is important, but you just can't keep improving what you've always done. There are times when you need to leapfrog, sometimes in products, sometimes in process, and other times both and may also include the entire business model. This is where the strategic framework in Figure 8.4 comes into play to align the organization and provide an

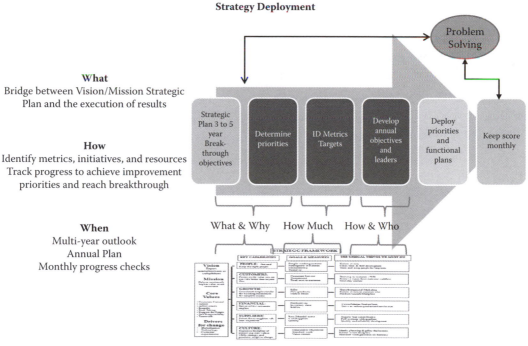

Figure 8.4   Strategy deployment.

environment to support innovation. In Lean it is called strategy deployment or policy deployment, like we mentioned in Chapters 3 and 5.

The term *policy deployment* may be unfamiliar and not intuitively obvious from its connotation. The words are a translation of the Japanese term Hoshin Kanri. In Japanese, Hoshin means "compass needle" or "direction." Kanri means "management" or "control." The name suggests how Hoshin planning aligns an organization toward accomplishing its strategic goal.

Hoshin Kanri is a management tool developed in the 1950s that became an integral part of how the Toyota Management System ultimately drives the company's performance. The discipline of Hoshin Kanri is intended to help an organization:

- Focus on a shared goal
- Communicate that goal to all leaders
- Involve all leaders in planning to achieve the goal
- Hold participants accountable for achieving their part of the plan

Bridge to Breakthrough Opportunities

It starts with a strategic plan and becomes the bridge from the company mission and vision to a multiyear strategy, sets the priorities, and guides organization execution on a daily, monthly, and annual timeline, usually down to each person's level. Starting at a 3- to 5-year strategic plan at a business company level, the management team works to identify where in that strategic plan it has true breakthrough opportunities to create real differentiation in how the business performs.

A breakthrough is an initiative that requires organizational stretch and represents a real game changer that customers value. It is a company initiative where it's not likely to involve only one function, the sales function or the R&D function or the administrative function, to get it done, but requires a cross-functional team. The company needs to align the entire organization in order to get there, and therefore a company needs to focus on just a few important initiatives.

The focus is on the target customer, the marketplace, and where there are opportunities for tremendous competitive advantage. Then the company must determine what needs to be built in order to be able to make the kind of progress that will lead to a 3- to 5-year breakthrough down the road. The strategic framework process then looks at those breakthroughs and steps them down into manageable initiatives and improvements that can be achieved during the first year of executing that plan. Monthly reviews are held to monitor progress, solve problems, and make adjustments as required.

Our example company, Amalgam, Inc., has a number of opportunities for improvement, and the management team decided the top three priorities are to:

1. Transform marketing and sales to drive customer value. The expectation is that this would differentiate the company in its chosen market and drive growth.
2. Streamline operations and reduce overall footprint. The expected result would be to improve service to customers by reducing lead times and improve margins.
3. Strengthen product development capabilities to create higher-value products and services. The expected outcome is that the company would have profitable differentiated value by adding products and services that customers would be willing to buy, even at premium pricing.

It was decided to approach the priorities in the above order, so we will review how Lean applies and supports each priority.

Using a similar approach, Price Industries has become a market leader in commercial HVAC, sheet metal, and plastics. Gerry Price, president and chief executive officer, presented its growth strategies at the Association for Manufacturing Excellence (AME) conference in Toronto in 2013. Starting the Lean journey in the mid-1990s, he described the business model that the E. H. Price team developed around their three fundamental objectives:

1. Making it easy for customers to do business with Price Industries. To that end, Price Industries developed its Rep Net program packed with innovative tools and industry first features. The Priceindustries.com web page is designed to simplify product selection, give designers greater access to resources, and make it easier than ever to do business with Price. It was designed to remove the waste from the design and product selection process as well as make orders error-free and shorten the order entry process.
2. Providing rapid, reliable, drumbeat delivery that customers can count on. They streamlined the operations flow to allow most items to be made to order, provide dependably short lead times, and on-time delivery.

3. Continuing relentless product development and product line expansion that allows offering more to customers. Their focus is to continuously improve existing products, as well as introduce entirely new product lines and highly differentiated, advanced technology products. Working with customers, Price validates project designs through firsthand witness testing using mock-ups and simulation rooms.

The punch line of Gerry's story is that during the 2009–2013 period, where commercial construction declined by almost 67%, Price Industries grew by 15% over that period.

Transforming Marketing and Sales

Amalgam, Inc.'s marketing and sales had been focused on the industrial and medical segments for years. The industrial segment had been declining and the medical segment growing slowly. Overall, Amalgam has experienced minimal growth, and profitability had been maintained with price increases in industrial business and some cost reductions. The medical segment has been under price pressure with group purchasing organizations (GPOs) representing multiple hospital groups and exerting strong price pressure through large-volume buys.

Amalgam's new CEO had been charged with growing the medical business where it was one of numerous players in the slow-growth, low-margin hospital supply business. Its sales structure was a traditional horizontal approach. A sales rep might call on hospitals, clinics, doctors' offices, etc. There's nothing fundamentally wrong with this approach, but it assumes that the customers know what they want and how to use it. This usually applies to commodity items, and when you are a commodity, you're not any different than "the other guy" down the street.

Growth previously was a lot about adding feet on the street, building capability in the sales team that created marginal growth, but was limited to cost and sales rep capacity. However, in recent years, Amalgam recognized that its customers had a growing array of new, higher-order needs that required different approaches to cover the market successfully. Health systems and hospitals had begun to expand their continuum of care within their market, and hospitals were vertically and horizontally diversifying their delivery systems. Additionally, healthcare providers like hospitals were caught between demands for quality care and growing cost pressures.

Amalgam realized that it served three different customer groups: hospitals, ambulatory centers, and physician groups. Within those groups in the United States, there are about 7,500 hospitals, 800 healthcare systems, 7,200 ambulatory surgery centers, and 180,000 physician groups. Within each group such as hospitals, there are subcategories such as the emergency room, intensive care unit, or operating room in the hospital. They buy Amalgam's type of products in different ways, some through distribution and others directly, and its products are consumables and not a capital investment.

So growth means acquiring new customers, finding out where they are, who the decision makers are, and educating them to make them aware of Amalgam, Inc., and that consumes a lot of a sales reps' time and effort. Most potential customers are currently using another company's product, so the sales rep needs to make contact and educate the decision makers in a way that Amalgam's products appear interesting and differentiated enough for them to think about Amalgam enough to possibly switch suppliers. Most people end up buying the same brand that they had in the past unless given a major reason to consider otherwise.

So how then does Amalgam drive growth? This is where marketing comes into play to drive growth. Without marketing, the business may offer the best products or services in the industry, but none of your potential customers would know about it. So, Amalgam put together a system that could be described as a transformative marketing approach. Within that system there are a number of Lean tools employed. Beginning with the voice of the customer (VOC), Amalgam redefined its product positioning, pared down its product lines, and focused its sales approach. Building on the VOC insights, Amalgam began to capitalize on a changing marketplace and, more importantly, the ability to begin providing new service offerings in multiple channels.

Using hospital and clinic directory data and known customer performance, Amalgam created a business model for each of the verticals and subverticals to define the products and estimate volume for each sales territory. Territories were aligned to the model, and a standard sales funnel management process was developed that could be cascaded out to the sales force. With that model it defined specific performance benchmarks to let everyone know just what good looked like. It facilitated the goal setting process from a traditional percentage growth target to a market model, and a way for the sales and marketing teams to track where they are vs. the benchmarks. Deploying this approach gave visibility of where the organization was vs. the goal to senior managers, regional management, and the individual rep, rapidly. This meant that Amalgam's sales and marketing would know what winning looks like for each particular part of the market.

With those benchmarks come visual management and daily management, which are really about helping teams track on a daily basis where they are vs. these benchmarks, so that they can drive performance improvements with knowledge.

Amalgam reported an average overall growth of 15% per year.

Some question the applicability of lean tools outside of operations. While Toyota for years has encouraged us to look beyond the production floor with their TPS other companies have found that lean tools are broadly applicable. As we have seen in Amalgam, organization can manage to improve their product and service development, their commercial activities as well as administration. Some examples include:

- Marketing – Drive customer preference with web lead generation program
- R & D – Change development from broadly used product/technology to vertical
- G & A – Use mapping to drive days outstanding and flag potential delinquencies.
- Strategic – Develop new business and whitespace penetration

A broader list is shown in Figure 8.5.

Streamline Operations and Reduce Overall Footprint

Amalgam, as we have seen, had developed a large number of redundant organizations and an asset footprint that was beyond the capacity required to operate successfully at a profit. The functional analysis shown in Figure 7.10 illustrated the original complex organization structure. Figure 8.6 shows the reduced structure. This provided clarity of how the operations would be structured and product locations.

The Amalgam operations team developed a Lean transformation model, and established a steering team to provide its site locations guidance on implementing Lean transitions in the factory and supply chain operations for its production systems. The model has four phases: (1) building a infrastructure to support Lean behavior, (2) redesigning the flow of products in the factory, (3) revamping the operations management, and (4) fostering process

Lean Management System Fundamental Tools

	Operations	R & D	Sales & Marketing	G & A
Voice of the Customer	Delivery Requirements	Product Requirement Specifications	Product positioning	People Development
Value Stream mapping	Cell Flow	Design Process	Lead handling	Accounts Receivable
Standard Work	Leader Standard Work	Engineering drawing and part selection	Sales funnel Management	Month end closing
Problem Solving Process	Quality Gap Reduction	Time to market Gap	Revenue Gap	Time to fill gaps
Transactional Process Improvement	Supplier Approval	Engineering Change Process cycle time	Copy/content Approval	Order entry
Kaizen		Time to Prototype	Whitespace Penetration	Empty seat
5S	Material Presentation	Design & Knowledge Retention library	End User Data Quality	Employee records
Visual & Daily Management	Cell Performance	Project progress and actions	Channel Performance	Customer Service Calls Status

Figure 8.5   Lean management system fundamental tools.

improvement. As a general guide for structuring a strategy for Lean implementation, the future state value stream map became the tool for planning and execution of the Lean transitions.

The customer service level and inventory reduction goals were set by the management team and deployed down through the organization through policy deployment. The initial efforts focused on the ERP (Electronic Requirements Planning) planning process and converting operations to a build-to-demand model to improve service levels. Bills of material were challenged and compressed. Lead times and lot sizes were cut.

Parallel efforts were begun within the various sites and production departments. Cellular manufacturing techniques were introduced to fabrication and assembly departments. Natural work teams planned and participated in creating product flow and area re-layouts. Flexibility was built in with benches and equipment on "wheels" and quick connects, so that all future layout modifications could be accommodated without complicated facility modifications.

Kanban controls were established within both the factory areas and supply chain. This eliminated many non-value-added reporting steps and stock room transactions and facilitated material replenishment as required. The supplier base was consolidated, providing material cost savings, and facilitated the move to supplier-managed inventory in many commodities. Shifts

FUTURE FUNCTIONAL MATRIX

DEPARTMENT/FUNCTION	NA LOCATIONS			EUROPE LOCATIONS				ASIA LOCATIONS		COUNT
	Cal 1	East 1	SA 1	Ger 1	Fr 1	Ir 1	Net 1	Aus 1	Chn 2	
CORPORATE	X			X		X			X	4
OPERATIONS										
Engineering/Sourcing	X				X	X				3
Quality	X	X	X	X	X	X			X	7
Purchasing/Planning	X	X		X	X	X				5
Manufacturing	X	X	X	X	X	X				6
Distribution	X	X		X	X			X		5
Product Refurbishment	X			X		X				3
Operation Reporting	X			X						2
FINANCE/ACCOUNTING										
Information Technology	X	X		X	X	X				5
Financial Analysis	X			X	X	X				4
Financial Reporting	X			X	X	X				4
Accounts Payable	X			X	X	X				4
Accounts Receivable/Collections	X			X	X	X				4
Manufacturing Cost Accounting	X			X	X	X				4
LEGAL										
Regulatory	X					X				2
Compliance	X					X				2
HUMAN RESOURCES	X	X		X	X	X				5
SALES/MARKETING										
Customer Service	X	X		X	X			X	X	6
Research & Development	X				X	X			X	4
Clinic WORKSHOP	X					X	X			3
Marketing	X			X	X	X			X	5
Sales	X	X		X	X			X	X	6
COUNT:	22	8	2	17	16	18	1	3	6	93

Figure 8.6 Future functional matrix.

were balanced to allow products to continue to flow across the entire process, and not just the bottleneck operations. Sequential inspection was initiated, followed by fail-safe steps.

Amalgam impact/results:

■ Inventory was reduced by 45%.

- Lead times were cut from 8 weeks to 5 days.
- First-pass failures were cut by 60%.
- On-time delivery went from near 80 to 97%.
- Product margins improved by 5 points.

This simplification and streamlining resulted in the freeing up of many resources (people, equipment, and space) for the planned growth opportunities.

Strengthen Product Development Capabilities

Amalgam, Inc.'s product development process followed a typical stage gate approach, which for the most part consisted of administrative checklists and controls, added cycle time, and lacked creative energy. The track record over the past few years had been few product releases, and those released were mostly variations of existing products, either their own or their competitors'. Innovation was at a standstill.

Lean had changed operations dramatically, but product development is both creative and process oriented. Does Lean apply in product development? Is one-piece flow also a state of perfection for product development? If we speed the process through the product development gates, is that any indicator of success? The output of any product development process is knowledge, as represented in the recipe, consisting of materials, how they go together, processing actions, and times. Lean doesn't look the same in development of products and services as it does in manufacturing, but yet the same principles apply.

Consider the typical product development process. Classic development practices would require engineering to define the requirements for the product before they designed it. Unfortunately, the requirements could not be known with certainty until the user (customer) experiences the product in its intended application and finds that it satisfies their needs. So, what do developers do? They make an educated guess of what the design requirements would be. Typically the developers are only partially correct, so redoing portions of design is a common occurrence.

Luckily Amalgam's competitors followed the same practice, so product managers look at development as follows: Did working with uncertain information cause expensive rework? Yes. However, the cost of the rework was small compared to the economic benefit of the cycle time savings and getting to market before competitors could take market share. Unfortunately for Amalgam, the new product flow was slow, and most lacked any real creativity to get customers' attention or differentiation. Consequently, the new products did not help Amalgam capture market share.

Amalgam sought to revitalize its product development process to strengthen product development capabilities in order to create higher-value products and services. The goal is to create profitable, differentiated value-adding products and services customers would be willing to buy at premium pricing to drive growth. This required a different thinking process about how to conceptualize, develop, and launch new products. Rather than the typical serial steps in the development process, Amalgam decided to follow the principles of Lean and start with the customer.

The design consulting company IDEO has described the process as design thinking. The design thinking process is best thought of as a system of overlapping spaces rather than a sequence of orderly steps, as we see in Figure 8.7. IDEO suggests there are three spaces to keep in mind: inspiration, ideation, and implementation.

- Inspiration is the problem or opportunity that motivates the search for solutions.
- Ideation is the process of generating, developing, and testing ideas.
- Implementation is the path that leads from the project stage into people's lives.

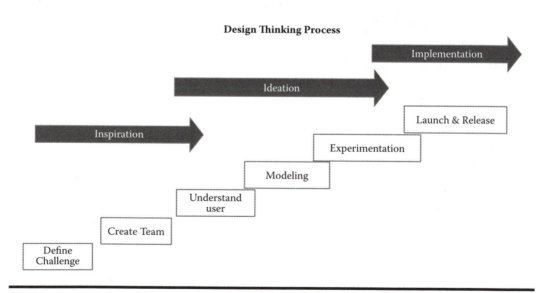

Figure 8.7 Design thinking process.

Amalgam started its journey by going to the Gemba. By connecting with its customers, the design team went to where the customer is and watched how they work and use supplied products. Once they understood the customer work processes, the customers and Amalgam developed value stream maps of the customer's workflow. The team identified the waste in their process, what was important to the customer, and what problems the customer had to work around to accomplish their objectives. This approach became the voice of the customer process and was conducted by small cross-functional teams ultimately in all target market segments.

The inspiration and ideation process and voice of the customer led them to look at the market differently. They conducted some open innovation workshops, conducted a search for new materials and suppliers, and created examples for the customers to see and try. A model for gathering customer feedback throughout the product development process is shown in Figure 8.8. Iterative prototyping is used to provide potential customers with something tangible to consider, experience, and comment on.

Most of the time customers cannot provide feedback or design input to something they have never seen, so most of the input is related to what they have seen or experienced. 3D modeling technology has really added a great tool to rapidly generate models that can be experienced by viewing,

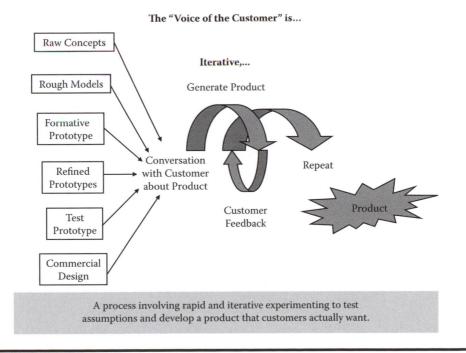

Figure 8.8   The "Voice of the Customer" is...

Chair Design Cycle of Learning

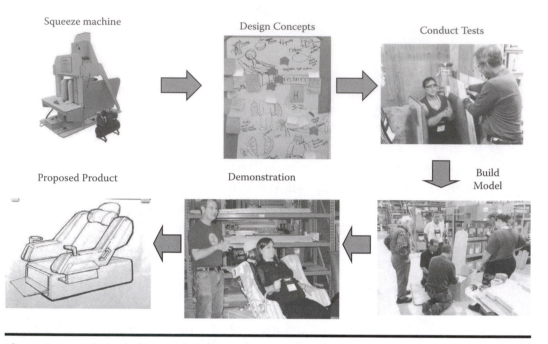

Figure 8.9   Chair design cycle of learning.

touching, and feeling prototypes by both the design team and the customers on a real-time basis.

Lean development teams eliminate wasted time and resources by developing the product iteratively and incrementally with a continuing dialog with the target customer.

In contrast to traditional product development, in which each stage occurs in linear order and lasts for months, Lean development builds products in short, rapid repeated cycles to speed the learning process. The team produces a product or sometimes a part of the product containing only critical features and gathers customer feedback.

The iterative design and dialog is really about failing early and failing fast, and it frontloads the product development cycle and prototyping. Previous experience in Amalgam was to spend months developing a prototype and then the next year or 2 years trying to make it work exactly like the team thought it should. The rapid modeling and customer involvement cycle might require multiple iterations and alternatives. By putting the cross-functional teams, including customers and suppliers, in one room, designs and alternatives are done in days. The steps shown in Figure 8.9 were actually 3 days' work by an AME-facilitated 3P (Production Preparation Process) workshop

Lean Project Planning Team

Building the Project Plan

Figure 8.10   Lean project planning team.

with the manufacturer, users, and AME members working on a redesign of the Squeeze Machine,* as originally designed by Temple Grandin.

Applying the principles of Lean to product development with visual management, the product plan and the launch plan and the development plan are all up on the wall (Figure 8.10) developed by the cross-functional team. The team works in a rapid Kaizen fashion to develop a macro project plan, which serves as the overall project plan. The project plan addresses the needs of the customer, the needs of the product and the needs of the business.

Once the plan is developed they conduct weekly and monthly reviews of the project diving into the detail planning as the project requires. While they're doing modeling, prototyping testing, and customer dialog, they are also mapping and building their supply chain and manufacturing processes. The objective is to be in a position by the time they get to manufacturing and launch to already know how to build it at the required rate to meet the projected demand.

In Figure 7.7, we saw how the new products contributed to the almost 15% annual growth in revenue for Amalgam.

What we have seen in Toyota, Danaher, Autoliv, and others, when Lean is adopted as a business system across the enterprise, it builds a

---

* Rapid Redesign of the Squeeze Machine through 3P, *Target*, vol. 28, no. 3, fall issue 2012.

robust growth company. It is time to end the tragedy, as Art Byrne put it, and begin to adopt Lean as a business strategy and management system. When we do that, the distinction of companies in manufacturing and nonmanufacturing sectors will become immaterial. Any company can benefit greatly.

Takeaways

1. Does everyone understand the company strategy? Is the strategy visible and practiced daily?
   a. Does the company mission make your job important?
   b. Does everyone know what is expected?
   c. Does everyone have the materials and equipment required to do their job?
   d. Are customers and their value requirements visible to everyone?

2. What is the breakthrough your company needs in technology, process, or business to significantly improve results?

3. What attributes of your company system relate to developing people and leadership?

4. Regarding your company's management system, do different departments have different systems or is there a companywide system?

5. How does your company management system support growth?

Chapter 9

Building Your Plan

"Would you tell me, please, which way I ought to go from here?"
    asked Alice
"That depends a good deal on where you want to get to," said the Cat.
"I don't much care where—" said Alice.
"Then it doesn't matter which way you go," said the Cat.

—Lewis Carroll, *Alice's Adventures in Wonderland* (1865)

No matter what level you are in the organization, by now you should be speaking the language of business. You should be able to answer the questions in Chapter 1 on sales, margins, total inventories, assets, and cash. In doing so, you are getting a picture of your company's total business performance. This doesn't take a lot of research, nor is it complicated, and is covered in public company quarterly and annual reports. For private company organizations, many owners don't share information because they believe their people don't understand or don't want to know. Most private company owners are usually willing to share information if there is a true indication of interest.

Let's look at the fundamentals of Apple, Inc.:

Apple reported fourth-quarter 2014 results on October 20, 2014. The company posted quarterly revenue of $42.1 billion and quarterly net profit of $8.5 billion, or $1.42 per diluted share. These results compare to revenue of $37.5 billion and net profit of $7.5 billion, or $1.18 per diluted share, in the year-ago quarter. Gross margin was 38 percent compared to 37 percent in the year-ago quarter. International sales accounted for 60 percent of the quarter's revenue.

Apple's board of directors has declared a cash dividend of $.47 per share of the Company's common stock. The dividend is payable on November 13, 2014, to shareholders of record as of the close of business on November 10, 2014.

"Our fiscal 2014 was one for the record books, including the biggest iPhone launch ever with iPhone 6 and iPhone 6 Plus," said Tim Cook, Apple's CEO. "With amazing innovations in our new iPhones, iPads and Macs, as well as iOS 8 and OS X Yosemite, we are heading into the holidays with Apple's strongest product lineup ever. We are also incredibly excited about Apple Watch and other great products and services in the pipeline for 2015."

"Our strong business performance drove EPS growth of 20 percent and a record $13.3 billion in cash flow from operations in the September quarter," said Luca Maestri, Apple's CFO. "We continued to execute aggressively against our capital return program, spending over $20 billion in the quarter and bringing cumulative returns to $94 billion."[*]

Now let's look at our made-up company Amalgam, Inc. before transformation:

■ Sales growing marginally through acquisition
■ Market share margins declining
■ Asset turns declining
■ Generating cash, but at lower rates than years before

Let's assume you worked for Amalgam prior to the transformation of the business and you knew the company had the capacity to generate cash, but lower than previous years, sales growth was not as good as the company would like, and asset turns were slowing. What would you do? Would you have a sense of urgency like our character Harvey on the burning platform in Chapter 4? You would have a better sense of what to focus on to address the business imparities that are, or should be, capturing the attention of the senior and board level management. You might look for ways to improve customer satisfaction and increase asset productivity. You might look for

---

[*] Apple press release, Oct. 20, 2014.

ways to improve product development of new products that create greater customer value and prospects for growth.

In the prior chapters, we have presented several company approaches to achieving successful transformation and moving on to becoming Lean for the long term, and the dramatic results that they have achieved. They have been successful because they have been able to adopt a Lean culture and management system across the enterprise, in all departments, functions, and divisions, and the discipline to stick with it as we have seen in Danaher, Toyota, Autoliv, and others. There have been many others that had good intentions and good results for a few years, but through changes of management direction, they drifted away or abandoned the limited Lean activities they had been doing.

Many of the concepts and Lean tools discussed in books and presentations describe significant results and are easy to do. Unfortunaately they have not had significant impact in business situations. Much of this is due to action plans that are sometimes too nebulous and not linked to the company business model, as we described in Chapter 7, or simply too limited in their application in the business. Building a plan that addresses the organizational needs and impacts performance must link to the total business model, the financials, and be actionable. As Womack and Jones explained in their book *Lean Thinking*[*]:

> There must be an action plan that real managers in real companies can deploy.

We agree—without a destination, any road will do, as the Cheshire Cat advised Alice. As we have learned from Steven Covey,[†] effective people begin with the end in mind. This does not mean necessarily that the end goal or vision is highly precise, but directive. This is based on imagination. All things are created from a mental creation, followed by a physical creation. Without a conscious effort to visualize your goals, other people and circumstances will shape the company by default. To begin with the end in mind means to begin with a clear vision of your desired direction and destination, and then act to make things happen. Becoming Lean is different than doing Lean. The idea of doing Lean, as if it is an activity to attach to existing operations, is a limiting application of the Lean principles. It is also

---

[*] James P. Womack and Daniel T. Jones, *LeanThinking*, Free Press, New York, 2003.
[†] Steven Covey, *The 7 Habits of Highly Effective People*, Simon & Schuster, New York, 2004.

reactive in nature. For example, we have a lengthy order entry process, so let's do a Kaizen event to improve the process. While not necessarily a bad thing to do, most of the time the blitz is the last improvement made to the process, and participants go back to their real jobs, and few if any improvements are made subsequently. The key, instead, is to become Lean. This is where companies differentiate themselves in the marketplace and adopt Lean for the long term.

Despite attempts, most businesses have not been able to capture or sustain the benefits of a Lean transformation. A Lean management system represents a fundamental change, and most businesses have pursued change in a tactical, rather than strategic, approach. Most failed Lean transformations that we found can be attributed to lack of true senior management commitment and understanding that becoming Lean is a process of organizational change. Additionally, the methodology many companies employ is a series of quick-hit approaches that deliver short-term benefits, but are not sustained in the longer term. Finally, we see a reluctance of many companies to address the business as a whole in their attempts with Lean, with a preference to concentrating on operations or manufacturing.

Roadmap to Lean Success

Building a roadmap or plan to becoming Lean obviously depends upon where you are in the organization and the progress the organization has made at the time you begin to create your plan. Figure 9.1 illustrates a high-level framework for building your plan. We call phase 0 the point at which you are at any given time you are creating or recreating your plan. It is not to say the organization has done nothing. In fact, since many companies are doing Lean stuff these days, you may have a lot to build on as you enter phase 0. The purpose of the phase 0 look is to clarify the business strategy and link the Lean development effort to the business model and the current business imparities that keep management up at night. These become the burning platform that can instill the urgency in the organization to act on the plan.

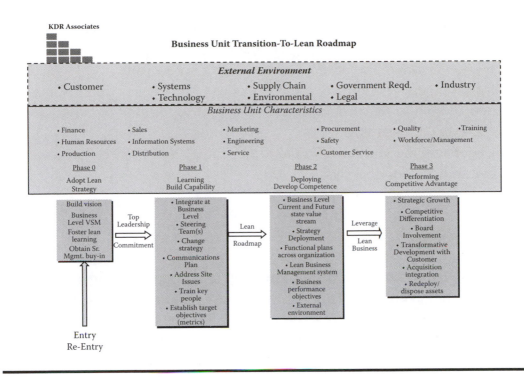

Figure 9.1 Business unit transition-to-Lean roadmap.

Key Drivers of Lean for the Long Term

Drawing from the successful companies such as Danaher, Autoliv, Toyota, and others, there are seven key drivers of Lean for the long term required for a business to become Lean, and they need to be part of building your plan:

1. Strategic leadership that understands Lean and the advantages of following the principles and adapting them within the company to achieve the business model.
2. Adopting a Lean focus at the business model level and challenging it to continually improve the customer experience and value delivery to achieve profitable growth.
3. Defining a uniquely branded Lean business system, as Danaher, Toyota, Honeywell, Pentair, and others have, as a commitment to Lean across the organization, defining how the business operates in all departments. We have called this a Lean management system.
4. Consistent communication of the vision, mission, values, and burning platform that propels the need to change and improve.

5. The correct infrastructure to support the business model and what is needed at the time to develop people in all departments to leverage the business competitive advantages the Lean efforts create.
6. Development over time of the continuous improvement and respect for people culture by coaching, mentoring, and supporting organizational and personal learning.
7. Understanding and drive for the Lean strategy and Lean culture's value by the board of directors.

1. Leadership

Once the Lean journey has been committed to by upper management, big steps must be taken. The plan of training and implementation needs to be laid out with the commitment to deploy from the top down. This includes analyzing the business model, key value streams, and scheduling when each of the departments is brought on board and defining what the expectations are.

In their *Harvard Business Review* article "The CEO's Role in Business Model Reinvention," Vijay Govindarajan and Chris Trimble[*] described some key concepts that should be addressed in phase 1 of learning and building capability in Lean. They studied the question "Why do established corporations struggle to find the next big thing before new competitors do?" The problem they tackled is pervasive and examples are countless. We noted Kodak as one glaring example of what they found to be a simple explanation of why this happens. Companies are too focused on executing the current business model and forget that every business model becomes obsolete at some time. Success today does not guarantee success tomorrow.

In Company X we saw that Lean is easily derailed with shifts in the leadership focus. Vijay Govindarajan and Chris Trimble demonstrated some of the reasons for this in their analysis of the CEO's Role in Business Model Reinvention. They summarized their findings in three-box model shown in Figure 9.2 which boils down to the following framework: manage the present, forget the past (selectively), and create the future.

---

[*] Vijay Govindarajan and Chris Trimble, The CEO's Role in Business Model Reinvention, *Harvard Business Review,* January 2011.

Three-Box Theory

	Box 1 *Managing the Present*	Box 2 *Selectively Forget the Past*	Box 3 *Create the Future*
	Normal everyday work:	*You must recognize that:*	*Long-term thinking:*
Strategy making	Data-driven results	Uncertainty is what creates opportunities. Some will feel threatened. It is easy to get stopped with "We tried that before."	Use breakthrough strategy deployment involving nontraditional players to create alternate and disruptive competitive advantages.
Accountability	Policy deployment develops strict accountability for results and a monthly cadence for follow-up and control	Past practices, technologies, and outmoded products can become a barrier to the future. Communication and knowledge sharing are vital to the organizational learning—lessons learned. New approaches may be required when the barriers arise.	True breakthrough initiatives are cross-functional. Teams need to be established to experiment and test hypotheses and assumptions about the future. This means evaluations are not based on short-term results, but on what the organization is learning from the experiments.
Organizational design	Perfect organizational alignment with the company goals through policy deployment and accountability	Old legacy organizations will feel threatened and will create obstacles to the future unless kept focused on present business. New alignment.	Start with the customer-driven business model shown in Figure 7.2 to build the organizational infrastructure of the future. Requires creative thinking and new units.

Figure 9.2 Three-box theory.

In box 1 it is important for the company to operate with organizational alignment for the core businesses to execute effectively. Companies that remain focused in box 1 however emphasizing only on cost reductions and Kaizens are managing in the present and vulnerable to changes in technologies, markets, and customer shifts.

In box 2 future trends and potential disruptions or nonlinear shifts are possible, but unknown. Here organizational diversity, creativity, innovation are vital and the biases, assumptions, and entrenched mind-sets that are typical of box 1 need to be challenged. Organizational alignment other than the recognition for the need to experiment and change can be dangerous to the health of the business.

In box 3 it's important to dedicate resources to future product and services, running experiments and working with current and future customers to chart the future course. This is the responsibility of upper management and depending on the scope may also be overseen by the board of directors.

Lean practitioners can add value in all three boxes, not just box 1.

Since we have noted the example of how Kodak failed to adjust with technology shifts Fujifilm, too, saw omens of digital doom as early as the 1980s. It developed a three-pronged strategy: to squeeze as much money out of the film business as possible, to prepare for the switch to digital and to develop new business lines. Fujifilm has mastered new tactics and survived. Film went from 60% of its profits in 2000 to basically nothing, yet it found new sources of revenue. Kodak, along with many a great company before it, appears simply to have run its course.[*]

The flexibility of the customer centric nature of a Lean culture and Lean practitioners should be leading disciplined experiments preparing the organization for the future. These experiments and the learning derived linked to the company business model and imperatives are what creates the initiatives for future business models. This is how Lean practitioner can add value in all three boxes, not just box 1 in making changes intended to improve today's business performance.

---

[*] The last Kodak moment?, *Economist* NEW YORK AND TOKYO print edition, Jan 14, 2012.

Leadership Team

The CEO/COO, president, and leadership team need to be brought on board early, as part of the long-term journey. They should be trained to develop skills in coaching and mentoring and make going to the Gemba standard work for them.

All leadership team members should become experts in some of the key Lean tools. It is not reasonable to expect anyone individual to be an expert in all the tools, but one or two related to their functions should be expected. Figure 9.3 illustrates some of the tools company leadership might assign to the functional managers. As experts, they would be expected to teak others in the company in the appropriate use and application of the tools.

Teaching classes is a great way for them to learn and show commitment and be visible! Serving on teams and working with employees to solve problems not only demonstrates leadership commitment, but also develops and demonstrates their skills to emulate.

The Lean philosophy should begin to make changes in all departments and addressed office work as part of the value streams to meet customers' needs. In the old bureaucratic management scheme, all departments were

Organizing for Lean

A good next step is to assign key functional heads a role as
a Lean Leader for one of the key tools of Lean

Functional Head	Lean Tool Focus
• Production Control Mgr.	➢ Kanban
• Purchasing Manager	➢ Point of Use Purchasing
• Quality Manager	➢ Poka-Yoke
• Maintenance Manager	➢ T.P.M. (total productive maint.)
• Manufacturing Eng. Mgr.	➢ S.M.E.D (set up reduction)
• Industrial Eng. Mgr.	➢ Standard Work
• Accounting Manager	➢ Administrative Kaizen
• Human Resources Mgr.	➢ Change Management
• Production Manager	➢ Visual Management
• Customer Care Mgr.	➢ Corrective action & 6 sigma
• Continuous Imp Mgr.	➢ Rapid Improvement events
• Sales/Marketing Mgr.	➢ Voice of the Customer

Figure 9.3   Organizing for Lean.

silos that looked out for their own interests, but not necessarily the customer's interests or the business's.

Texas Instruments (TI) realized this was a problem and conducted a management experiment to shift the organization to value stream managers as an overlay to the normal departments and functional management chart. For instance, the vice president of manufacturing was put in charge and became manager of the "product production process" value stream. The value stream began when they received a contract order and ended upon delivery to the contract requirements, including all warranty processes. So this tied the engineering, drafting, configuration management, purchasing, inspection, kitting, fabrication, assembly, testing, and shipping departments and their processes under one value stream manager. He managed by monitoring the processes and performance metrics, including cycle time, handoffs, duplicate steps, costs, and quality indices. This was a major change in leadership's mindset and helped focus on the customer and value added in a Lean manner rather than the traditional financial metrics. In the Dupont model introduced in Chapter 2, Value Stream Leaders monitor and work the non-financial drivers to get results.

Phil Roether, who was the vice president of Manufacturing and manager of the product production process, described that TI's Defense Systems and Electronics Group (DSEG), which had won the Malcolm Baldrige National Quality Award in 1992, had targeted a strategy of speed to market as a differentiator strategy. So the product production process became the vehicle to outperform the competition. Their lead time was 18 months from contract award to prototype delivery. By reducing that to 6 months, which would be customer focused, their proposals could also eliminate the "progress payments" element to the contract. This was another customer benefit—less administration and cash flow! Specific details included reducing the order entry cycle time from 14 weeks to 3 days, with approval signatures cut from 14 to 2. The circuit card design process had been trimmed from greater than 6 months to 90 days using standard parts and standard designs.

By reducing cycle time for design and production, they received many new contracts.

One was awarded to TI because the governmental agency (not the United States) found it had a need in March and the $20 million funding was good until May. TI delivered! A follow-on award of $20 million brought the total business benefit to $40 million based on the cycle time reduction! TI DSEG had about a 2% growth in 1996, which exceeded the growth of all other defense businesses. One of their customers was quoted as saying, "TI is the most business progressive and could be called the Toyota of Defense businesses!"

Phil left us with a quote of his own:

"What Leadership wants, Leadership gets!"*

The learning we take away here is to be careful what you want. If management is focused on the right things, they will make the right things happen.

Changing Leadership Trends

As indicated in *Lean Thinking*,† Womack and Jones found that early on, many of the Lean transformations were instigated and promoted by management CEOs with passionate leadership ability that was needed to overcome the old-style bureaucratic corporate inertia. More recently, however, they have seen mid-level managers, including Lean practitioners, take the lead. Also in *Strategic Transformation*,‡ Hensman, Johnson, and Yip came to the same conclusions based on their research in the UK that covered companies that have been consistently successful for the last 20 to 25 years. They identified the dangers of a leader who acted as an autocrat, however well intended. They found coalitions of managers were formed informally that really made things happen to address the business model aggressively. These coalitions created a constructive tension with internal debates, uncomfortable as that may be, that created good sounding boards for better thought out approaches to the business model and collaborative problem solving.

2. Focus on the Business Model

By focusing on the customer and the value-delivery process in the business model, as we stated in Chapter 7, we showed that the business model needed a major overhaul to address customer needs and Amalgam's assignment of limited resources. There clearly was not alignment, and many resources were providing little to no value. With a strategic Lean transformation plan, the company will see that Lean in all areas is a process of building capability, developing competence to perform at a level that achieves a competitive advantage. This is a long-term commitment. As we illustrated

---

* Interview with Phil Roether, July 24, 2014.
† Lean Thinking, James P. Womack and Daniel T. Jones, Free Press, 1996, 3003, New York, N.Y.
‡ Manual Hensman, Gerry Johnson, and George Yip, *Strategic Transformation: Changing while Winning*, Palgrave McMillan, St. Martins Press, New York, 2013.

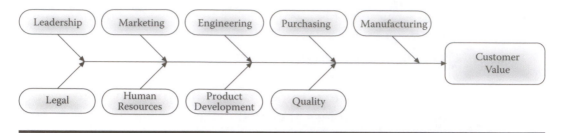

Figure 9.4   Major components of the total cost structure of Amalgam, Inc.

in Chapter 7, the Amalgam, Inc. cost structure shown in Figure 7.1 identifies that all departments contribute to the Lean organization and customer value, although they may have stayed out of the fray previously. Chapter 8 illustrated how Lean applies across the organization, and while cost is a consideration, Lean actually becomes a growth strategy. It also shows that there may be several components much larger than manufacturing costs that should be addressed in a Lean organization strategy, as we showed in our Amalgam, Inc. example. This can also be depicted in a traditional fishbone diagram (Figure 9.4).

With the leadership team's support and actions this can be done; it just takes changes to the customary departmental thinking. Using the Lean principles in all these departments may seem out of the ordinary the first few years, but that is exactly what a long-term Lean company does! Management's expectations that these are companywide tools and philosophy must be consistent and demonstrated with frequent standard work trips to the office Gemba, as well as the manufacturing Gemba.

The business model must be continually reevaluated in light of the customer, the technology, changing demographics, and resources deployment. The Lean practitioner should be working with upper management to use Lean tools to analyze and provide the factual data to make the best decisions. This also offers a much higher impact and appreciation of the Lean strategy, rather than running small Kaizens on the factory floor.

3. Lean across the Organization

The Lean Journey—Understanding It's a Long Journey and There Will Be Culture Change for All

We researched a number of organizations' approaches to Lean transformation and noted a number of different strategies based on very different assumptions about the different forces facing the leaders. Plans were identified for transforming the enterprise end to end, as with Danaher over the past 25 years, to achieve huge returns on investment, and on the other hand, highly focused efforts in Amalgam to energize the company's growth. In others we noted, such as Company X, which went deep into operations excellence, avoiding the leadership, marketing, sales, and administrative functions, and then experiencing a leadership change that derailed the Lean efforts and also derailed the company performance. We saw some companies approach Lean by learning in small beta test model areas, and others in a series of rapid Kaizen events to improve things scattered here and there in the organization.

Company leadership is charged with delivering results, and many times must do it quickly. In this case, they must balance the desire for speedy results with the Lean journey to systematically improve processes and develop people's improvement capability.

Obviously all company situations require different strategies, so there is no pat answer, but sometimes disruptive actions need to be done because of where the company is at that point in time. Toyota has had some disruptions, but none that would seem like what we see in industry consolidations such as the Kodak photo technology shift and the Apple iPad and iPhone explosion.

There are many books describing the Lean transformation and the successes. There are also many companies that have achieved marginal success and less than they expected. The top 10 Lean failure modes are listed in Chapter 3 with suggested counteractions to take when you see a failure mode developing. We believe that an ongoing plan that evolves and creates institutionalized Lean should be the basis of the transformation in the first place—not just cost savings on myriad projects or just a continuous improvement strategy in manufacturing. These are programs, projects, or flavors of the month and will not be around for very long.

The three phases of institutionalizing Lean are our Lean management maturity tool to provide insight and a benchmark to evaluate progress as companies strive to achieve institutionalized Lean as we described above. In Figure 9.5 we've outlined the three phases of institutionalized Lean within the company that need to be the basis of the Lean journey plan.

Phase 1: Use of Continuous Improvement Tools and Systems

Based on the needs of the business identified in the value stream analysis and business model, initial activities need to be selected to introduce Lean

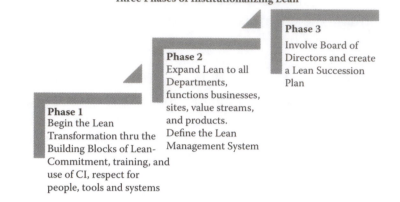

Three Phases of Institutionalizing Lean

Phase 3
Involve Board of Directors and create a Lean Succession Plan

Phase 2
Expand Lean to all Departments, functions businesses, sites, value streams, and products. Define the Lean Management System

Phase 1
Begin the Lean Transformation thru the Building Blocks of Lean- Commitment, training, and use of CI, respect for people, tools and systems

Figure 9.5   Three phases of institutionalizing Lean.

thinking and the long-term journey ahead. The needs of the business are top priority, and by using Lean tools to identify real major improvement areas, we can reinforce the strong link between Lean and all business process improvements. This should include high-priority processes and visible activities.

What we see is that many companies are picking Kaizens to study and improve problem areas for quick successes from the low-hanging fruit, and also using 5S in all work cells and offices to raise individual awareness. These approaches can be a good start, but by no means should they be the only activities. In addition to quick short-term successes, we are trying to demonstrate that continuous improvement and respect for people are the building blocks for the long term. This is considered a necessary step, but not sufficient, as we see in phases 2 and 3.

Caution: In phase 1 is where most companies on the Lean journey reside and stagnate. The focus is on continuous improvement in manufacturing and cost savings. There is a lot of low-hanging fruit, and everyone can become excited on the progress and cost savings produced. From the CEO's standpoint, this is where he or she can point to, in order to validate the decision to begin the journey in the first place. Sometimes this phase can last for 5 to 8 years with great results, but with little attention paid to phases 2 and 3. In most cases, this initial phase is in the manufacturing arena because it's easy to concentrate on reducing materials cost and direct labor hours. After all, we've been doing this since Henry Ford's River Rouge plant, and the manufacturing folks are trained to think in those terms. The initial Lean practitioners often concentrate here to gain traction and show quick results. In this phase there is concern regarding how we deploy these tools and help everyone use them in their standard work. Most often a core group of Lean practitioners is charted, recruited, trained, and deployed to lead and mentor others. Let's look at some examples.

As the early cost savings are recognized, everyone can become satisfied with the Lean transformation since they have seen that the results are good. Too often, however, that is the only goal of Lean: cost savings. After some time, maybe 4 to 8 years, the low-hanging fruit is not as plentiful as it once was and the CEO may think the benefits from doing Lean have dissipated and he or she needs to look for a new approach. "What's next? Is there a new management theory that I need to try to show I am on the cutting edge?" This can be a real temptation to upper management. But the real question that needs to be asked is, "Have we expanded the role of Lean to all business functions, plants, products, and levels of management?" Are managers mentoring and going to the Gemba (workplace) to learn and experiment in order to achieve continuous improvement? Have we defined a Lean management system that involves Lean thinking in all aspects of the business, and does everyone realize that Lean is the long-term approach to managing the company?

Phase 2a: Lean Management System

An institutionalized Lean management system (LMS), as discussed in Chapters 2, 3, 4, and 6, incorporates all the elements of continuous improvement, along with respect for people at all levels and in all departments and separate businesses and plants, but must support the business model to be successful.

Figure 9.6 is a repeat of Figure 2.6 and Figure 8.2. We feel it to be a central definition of the key elements to a Lean management system. It outlines the five elements of a Lean management system: clarity of purpose, standard work, transparency, accountability, and innovation. It's focused on the customers and works continuously to involve and align the entire organization in relation to the business model. Lean will also challenge the business model to continually be responsive to the customers and changing market conditions.

We talked earlier in Chapters 4 and 6 about the importance of the Lean management systems installed by the leaders of Lean that have prevailed for the long term: Ford, Autoliv, Hillenbrand, and Danaher, all modeled after the Toyota Production System, but adapted to their company. The LMS they publicly advertise and use makes no mistake about their expectations of how to run the business and that it's their strategic weapon of choice. By adopting a LMS, they have committed from the top down, including the board,

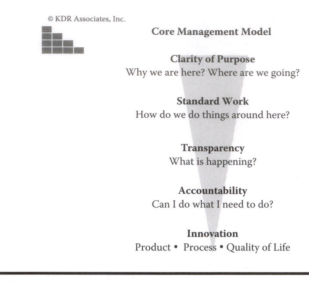

© KDR Associates, Inc.

Core Management Model

Clarity of Purpose
Why we are here? Where are we going?

Standard Work
How do we do things around here?

Transparency
What is happening?

Accountability
Can I do what I need to do?

Innovation
Product • Process • Quality of Life

Figure 9.6   Core management model.

that addressing customer value by continuous improvement and respect for people is the way of their future.

A great example, but one that is not necessarily long term yet, is ShawCor. This offers great insight on building a transformation plan and progressing through each of the three phases highlighted in Figures 9.1 and 9.5. ShawCor is now in its 50th year as a public company. It began as a specialty pipe coater in Ontario, Canada and has since grown into a global energy pipeline and services company with manufacturing and service facilities in fifteen countries. Its workforce includes over 8,000 employees operating in more than 25 countries worldwide. They draw on the global talent pool and most of the company's facilities are operated by local and regional employees.

In 2006 ShawCor launched what is now termed as the ShawCor Management System (SMS). Initially it was launched as the ShawCor Manufacturing System and deployed across all manufacturing facilities. The company says the SMS has played a key role in the development of strong supportive leadership and fostered a culture that is innovative and adaptive to the market and their customers. They see SMS as a way to counter increased global competition, enable growth and their drive for a long term sustainable competitive advantage.

In 2012 the company expanded the scope to an enterprise wide vision giving way to the ShawCor Management System. It was a strategic decision for the organization. With a global SMS, aligned operations and top level leadership ShawCor has made the application of SMS a way of life. It

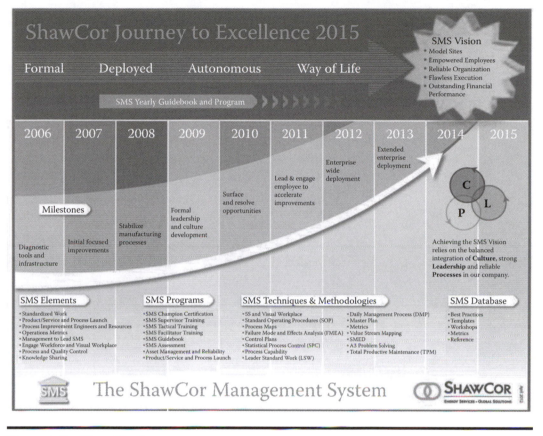

Figure 9.7   ShawCor Journey.

established a coherent strategy, vision and purpose for the 8,000 employees. ShawCor has described their journey so far in the illustration in Figure 9.7. Their dramatic stock performance is shown in Figure 9.8 and a summary of important financial indices is shown in Figure 9.9. Although only on a 9-year journey so far they are well on their way to success through Lean for the long term.

All these companies that have been successful over the long term publicly advertise and use a LMS. They make no mistake about their expectations of how to run the business and that Lean is their strategic weapon of choice. By adopting a LMS they have committed from the top down, including the board, that addressing customer value through a focus on continuous improvement and respect for people is the way of the future. Here, by the way, continuous improvement involves challenging the business model and customer future expectations. New technology may be about to burst the current model, and past trends may not survive in the future. The fact that the LMS is installed

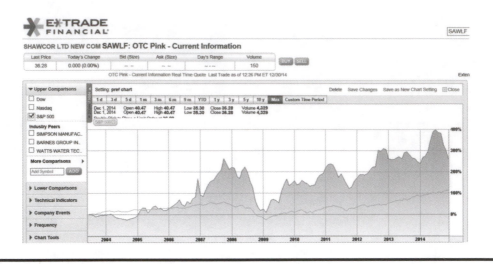

Figure 9.8   ShawCor stock performance.

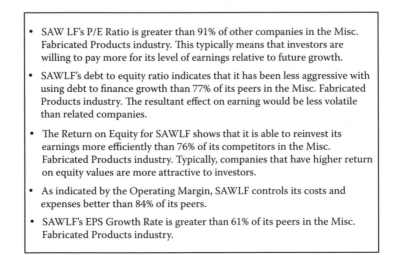

Figure 9.9   ShawCor financial indices.

also defines, to a more permanent degree, the expectations in succession planning for any newly appointed CEO, president, or upper management. The LMS also needs to be embedded in the HR policies, procedures, and career planning process and the performance review system. All HR activities, such as idea programs and reward and recognition programs, need to be aligned with the LMS. What gets measured gets done!

Phase 2b: Expand Lean and Involve the Entire Organization

With a longer-term strategic Lean transformation plan, the company will see that Lean in all areas is a very long-term journey. As we stated in Chapter 7, the Amalgam, Inc. cost structure shown in Figure 7.1 identifies that all departments contribute to the Lean organization, cost structure, and customer value, although they may have stayed out of the fray previously. Chapter 8 illustrated how Lean applies across the organization, and while cost is a consideration, Lean actually becomes a growth strategy. It also shows that there may be several components much larger than manufacturing costs that should be addressed in a Lean organization strategy, as we showed in our Amalgam, Inc. example.

With the leadership team's support and actions this can be done; it just takes changes to the customary departmental thinking. Using the Lean principles in all these departments may seem out of the ordinary the first few years, but that is exactly what a long-term Lean company does! Management's expectations that these are companywide tools and philosophy must be consistent and demonstrated with frequent standard work trips to the office Gemba, as well as the manufacturing Gemba.

A Lean practitioner can be trained within the department to be the Lean champion as part of the department leadership team. The Lean practitioner will need to report at a high level in order to gain respect, and also must have the confidence of the departmental manager that he or she is there to help. The Lean practitioner will need mastery of the tools, but more importantly, understand the value proposition and business model of the company. High-level, major impact activities are the value-added benefit here, not small inconsequential projects that take no risk! By identifying potential risk and reward and understanding the resources required that we identified in Chapter 6, the Lean practitioner can lead the upper division/department manager to support Lean in a whole new way.

Phase 3: Involving the Board of Directors

Refer to key driver number 7—"Lean Strategy and Interfacing with the Board of Directors"—below.

4. Consistent Communications

As part of the long-term journey upper management needs to provide consistent, clear communications so that all employees have no doubt of where the company is going and what the expectations are. They want and need to know about their personal future and the future path of the company. Everyone wants to be considered an insider. This is key to the basic building block of Lean: respect for people.

The basis of the company is defined by upper management in the vision, mission, and values that are very public. The true determinant of building trust is if the actions of upper management support what they are saying!

Clear communications are needed to support the Lean journey to address:

■ Why are we doing this and where do we need to go?
■ Is there a burning platform? Is there an industry benchmark or trend that we can point to? Is there urgency?
■ If some restructuring is required, that should be dealt with before embarking on something that affects people and their jobs.

Some companies list Lean as their management system and strategy in their annual report and on their website to drive a stake in the ground and leave no doubt about their expectations.

5. Lean Infrastructure

Lean Staffing Organization

Establishment of a Lean practitioner system will need to be designed. Depending on the organization, it might start as a central group or a dispersed group working to the same training and continuous improvement standard processes. Either way, the knowledge of continuous improvement tools and coaching individuals needs to be shared and expanded.

Many companies establish a Lean office or, as we used earlier, a Lean promotion office to help deploy Lean throughout the company, but unfortunately, these Lean practitioners are often located too low in the organization and are not granted a strategic position that has the ear of the CEO and upper management. They generally do a good job of what is asked of them—generate cost savings in manufacturing. We have to think of Lean as a strategic tool for the long term.

Raytheon used Raytheon Six Sigma™ (R6S) experts. They were change agent practitioners, trained in Lean, Six Sigma, and change management skills and tools and validated to be effective at the Black Belt level. After numerous successful projects and demonstrating leadership skills, they were nominated by their business leader to be designated an R6S expert. At this point, they were personally interviewed by the CEO, Dan Burnham, before being certified and assigned. Initially they all reported to a corporate office and were allocated to the various businesses. As the businesses and the transformation matured, each business president selected a lead business Raytheon Six Sigma master expert to serve on his staff. This provided Lean practitioners at the top level in each business that could look at strategic processes to drive the business improvements, and they had the ear of their business president. There were also R6S experts and change agents that indirectly reported to the business lead to promote standard work and communication to facilitate business changes.

It's important that the deployment of Lean practitioners be carefully planned and be in alignment with the company businesses and culture to achieve the long-term benefits. The more they are part of the business management leadership team, the better.

Insertion of the Lean Practitioner into the Business

If there is no Lean management system in place, the Lean practitioner may have to work on a plan to become involved in what may be considered a business problem, not a manufacturing one. To do this in a small company requires gaining the ear of someone in upper management and volunteering to help by gathering data for management to analyze or to work on a team to pull it together. With the Lean tool expertise, he or she will be in a prime position to learn and become familiar with the business process and data. The Lean practitioner may not be asked to analyze the data (that may be reserved for upper management), but providing insight using models similar to those we illustrated for Amalgam and using the language of the business that we highlighted in Chapter 1 may be an acceptable role. Working within the unique company culture can be sensitive and tricky, but gathering facts and data can solidify trust and competence and future personal value to the company and the managers involved. If the Lean practitioner is a respected and fast-track employee, this will not be a major hurdle.

In larger companies with many sites, the Lean practitioner's plan may be a little different. He or she may be in a remote site or function and not have access to upper management. In this case the approach can be similar. First steps could be to locate a senior mentor that can help you become exposed to many different projects. The Lean practitioner should study the business, look for opportunities to make a large impact and volunteer ideas and put in extra effort to establish a track record of broad business and lean knowledge. Again, using the Lean approach and expertise with Lean tools, the Lean practitioner's goal is to establish himself or herself as a business-savvy Lean practitioner that can be counted on to add value in any situation. Of course, this takes a bit of personal risk and may require extra work as you establish yourself and your positive reputation, but the payback is great for the individual and the company!

6. Development of Culture

Understanding It's a Long Journey and There Will Be Culture Change for All

We researched a number of organizations' approaches to Lean transformation and noted a number of different strategies based on very different assumptions about the different forces facing the leaders. We identified plans for transforming the enterprise end to end, as with Danaher over the past 25 years, to achieve huge returns on investment, and on the other hand, highly focused efforts in Amalgam to energize the company's growth. In others we noted, such as Company X, which went deep into operations excellence, avoiding the leadership, marketing, sales, and administrative functions, and then experiencing a leadership change that derailed the Lean efforts and also derailed the company performance. We saw some companies approach Lean by learning in small beta test model areas, and others in a series of rapid Kaizen events to improve things scattered here and there in the organization.

Company leadership is charged with delivering results, and many times must do it quickly. In this case, they must balance the desire for speedy results with the Lean journey to systematically improve processes and develop people's improvement capability.

Obviously all company situations require different strategies, so there is no pat answer, but sometimes disruptive actions need to be done because of where the company is at that point in time. Toyota has had some disruptions, but none that would seem like what we see in industry consolidations such as the Kodak photo technology shift and the Apple iPad and iPhone explosion. Layer 3 of evolutionary capability, discussed by Taka Fujimoto below, which includes strategic breakthroughs and innovation discussed earlier, must be fully part of the successful company's strategy and Lean management plan.

Once the CEO or upper management begins a Lean transformation journey, it's incumbent that they understand it's a culture change for both short-term and long-term benefits. If there are no Lean practitioners per se, there may be other change agents or continuous improvement specialists in the organization. A big breakthrough opportunity is for management to believe it is a major cultural undertaking and not a project or initiative. In the beginning, it may be the manufacturing manager or operations manager that has the most understanding, or it could come from a benchmarking visit or a Lean consultant that has the ear of the CEO. One of the better Lean transformations was led by the chief financial officer. It would be very helpful if knowledge of the organizational and personal changes required were explained and understood by all upper management. The source of knowledge can come from reading, such as this book and others, but is more impactful by benchmarking face-to-face with some of the successful long-term success stories and asking questions.

Organizational Learning in the Culture

A successful Lean transformation needs to recognize there are both an individual and an organizational learning aspect in the culture change. Earlier we discussed Peter Senge's three levels of developing a shared vision in Chapter 4 to show there are progressions in a learning organization. Let's reuse that as we examine Toyota's approach to organizational capability, which is a progression to achieve organizational capability through continuous learning.

Taka Fujimoto, the foremost scholar of Toyota in Japan,[*] distinguishes between competing through price or product and competing through organizational capability, and identifies organizational capability as a key element

---

[*] Takahiro Fujimoto, *Competing to Be Really, Really Good*, International House of Japan, Minato-Ku, Tokyo, 2007.

in long-term success. His view of organizational capability in regard to manufacturing comprises three layers:

1. The base layer is routine manufacturing capability. That is the capability of producing the same product as competitors at lower cost, at higher quality, and with shorter delivery lead time. Better machines, better trained people, and a good company working environment all contribute to this traditional approach.
2. The second layer is routine continuous improvement capability—the ability to achieve continuous improvements (Kaizens), usually in productivity, quality, delivery lead times, and safety, generating more customer value. It is the capacity and cultural expectation to undertake problem-solving cycles continually, driving relentless improvement in products and services.
3. The third layer: evolutionary capability is capability-building capability. That capability is anything but routine; it is the capacity for developing new capabilities out of organizational chaos. This can be characterized as innovation by seeing new markets and technologies and linking them with new customer unstated needs.

Lean practitioners and upper management should be in tune with these three layers of organizational capability to develop the organization and make them a competitive advantage.

Time Allocation—Your Most Precious Resource

As we looked at resource allocation we found the organization's time allocation to be a major factor on what gets done on a day-to-day basis, and it ties directly to the three layers of organizational capability above. Daily management must be done, but should be a relatively small portion of upper management's focus. Kaizens focused on major changes constitute a good portion of mid-management's time, but upper management will be working on strategic breakthroughs that help drive the long-term success of the company, as depicted in Figure 9.10.

One caution: Continuous improvement and Kaizen events will *not* sustain a company for the long term. Strategic breakthroughs must be part of the Lean culture that Toyota modeled in Figure 9.10. Taka Fujimoto's third layer of evolutionary capability, discussed above (we may call innovation), is very important since the company must look for growth and new opportunities for customer value through strategic breakthroughs.

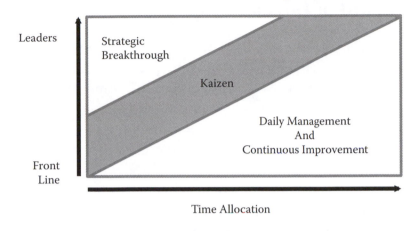

Figure 9.10 Three levels of improvement and time allocation.

A Lean management system is one that maintains a consistent focus on creating customer value, as well as on the processes the company uses to create and deliver that value. That is the main ingredient to creating wealth.

> In our evolutionary past, whoever thought too long and hard vanished inside the predator's jaws.*
>
> **—Rolf Dobelli**

This quote brings up another key tenant of Lean: to be action oriented and not spend too much time on the planning phase since all planning has errors. It is best to continually run experiments that generate learning and quick failures that can be overcome rapidly to deliver the customer value. So the Lean culture needs to include these aspects:

- Run experiments
- Learn from failure
- Be action oriented

* Rolf Dobelli, *The Art of Thinking Clearly*, HarperCollins, New York, 2013.

7. Lean Strategy and Interfacing with the Board of Directors

This key driver also represents phase 3 of institutionalizing Lean, as depicted in Figure 9.5. Depending on the company, of course, the board of directors needs to be involved and aware of the company culture that is under their oversight. Results only happen if the culture is aligned with the goals of the leadership, and this is a very important aspect of future performance. When the board understands the Lean aspects that they are endorsing, they will be more knowledgeable of the whats, hows, and whys. For instance, does the policy deployment system (Hoshin planning) effectively describe the company goals and gain employee commitment to attain them? Will the company culture fit with a new leader? In the old approach to leadership, the board may hire a successful leader from outside the company that did well in another industry and expect similar results. But in today's world, "hope" is not a plan and the board needs to be aware of and review any new management approach to confirm its validity and applicability to the current company culture and the projected impact of any major change to how the company operates. We know this may be asking a lot of the board compared to prior expectations of them. A major contributing factor is the speed of business in the 21st century and the Internet world that has changed everything. From the board's perspective, we must focus on the customer and be tuned to continuous improvement and using our people's talents in new and exciting ways. This is our burning platform.

In a Lean transformation, the highest-ranking Lean practitioner or Lean management champion needs to work with others in upper management and the CEO to suggest the board be briefed and understand and support the Lean journey. The CEO/president may have already briefed the board, but like most change efforts, as referenced in Chapter 3, about 20% of the board will be early adopters, 60% fence sitters, and 20% foot draggers. The board needs to become comfortable with the Lean culture and see the short-term and long-term benefits. The CEO and leadership team should be active salesmen and produce results to bring the board "on board." A visionary Lean leader will see this as a requirement per Alan Mulally of Ford, as discussed in Chapter 6, but the Lean practitioners must assist when and where they see a need!

The other question to ask is: Is there a succession plan for a new Lean leader? This can be easily addressed if the CEO grooms qualified successors that are deeply involved in Lean already. Again, Mullaly of Ford saw to it that he mentored and coached his planned replacement, so that the successor was a Lean believer trained in all aspects when he retired. If there is no internal leader being groomed, this is a definite sign that the Lean transformation may not survive.

The best way to predict your future is to create it.

—Abraham Lincoln

Framing Your Plan

The chaos of opinions created by the hype and buzzwords around best practices is unfortunate. Often overlooked is the confluence of other critical factors, such as company culture, employee behaviors, and preexisting infrastructure, which are pivotal to success. Transformation plans that simply attempt to apply best practices can easily turn the desire for bold, systemic change into a rag-tag collection of discrete, ad hoc initiatives. Such approaches can also prevent the kind of meaningful discussion that keeps a management group from pulling together toward a common end.

Transformation means change. Change in the right direction is improvement. Experience indicates that no single type of "magic pill" change initiative is sufficient to bring about acceptable levels of performance improvement for every business. Consequently, each company's program including yours is unique. There are, however, four common dimensions of change programs that should be considered in developing the Lean Transformation plan for your unique company or business. Successful long-term efforts develop points of view on all four. Where any one dimension is absent, the ill-matched collection of initiatives under way will fall short. Poor results are invariably the result of focusing efforts along only one or two—rather than all four—of the key axes of change illustrated in Figure 9.11:

1. Top-Down Direction.

Fundamentally any transformation effort must clearly answer the questions: "What problem are we trying to solve?" and "What kind of leadership behavior do we need?" This is derived from top-down direction setting to create focus throughout an organization which develops the conditions for performance improvement. This is emphasized in the Lean management system through Figure 9.11 Dimensions of Change creating clarity of purpose.

Key Changes Axes for Planning

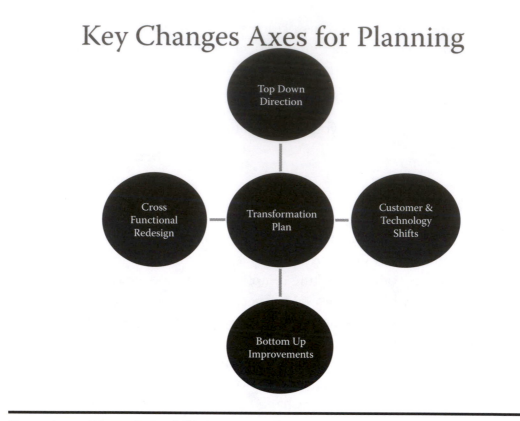

Figure 9.11   Dimensions of change.

2. Bottom-up Improvements.

Broad-based, bottom-up performance improvement requires getting people at all levels involved to take a fresh approach to solving problems and improving performance. This requires exploring the questions: "What capabilities are required at all levels in the organization? and "How will we develop the people to be able to solve the problems?" The elements of Standard Work, Transparency and Accountability support this axis along with establishing a common problem solving methodology.

3. Cross-functional Redesign.

Core processes link activities, functions, and information. Addressing these in new ways to achieve breakthrough improvements in cost, quality, and timeliness requires cross-functional teams to bring the innovation element to the forefront. The question to answer in this dimension is; "How should/will we improve the value delivery system or value creating work?" Value Stream Mapping may be one of the lean tools employed in this axis.

4. Customer and Technology Shifts.

External shifts that threaten core business or present new opportunities in the type of or the way business currently operates must be constantly on the radar screen. Here we suggest exploring the driver for transformation. Answer the questions: "What is driving the transformation?" For example is it driven by an implementation mindset that requires rolling out known improvement tools?" or "Is the transformation driven by shifts in technology, market, or customer requirements that require more experimental and scientific learning?" Lean tools such as Voice of the Customer and Technology Road Mapping may be a good choice of tools in this dimension.

Together, these four axes make up a balanced, integrated framework for combining separate initiatives into a coherent overall transformation plan. Most companies start with very broad objectives such as, "to lead the industry in customer satisfaction." But this is like saying "sail east" as a direction for sailing from Miami to Jamaica. Successful efforts strive over time for increasing clarity and specificity in top-down direction as change becomes more tangible throughout the organization. The broad objective may be refined to something like, "to be the easiest to work with at every customer interaction." The strategic framework we introduced in chapter 4 is a good start to bring focus to the company efforts.

Although top-down efforts create the focus and the necessary preconditions for transformational change, they alone are not sufficient to achieve it. Management needs to overcome the widely held view that "all we have to do is tell employees what we want, provide some training and rewards, and change will happen." This approach may work when the desired results lie well within the existing capabilities of an organization such as rearranging the production floor. It is insufficient when the change requires fundamentally new ways of doing business such as entering new markets or moving to a solution focus from product focus. In these cases, embedded skills, systems, and attitudes may actually be at odds with the new requirements. The three box analysis and focus setting process illustrated in Figure 9.2 can help identify in which organizational change arena you are playing and the approach to take.

So to be truly effective, the approach employed must be tailored to the specific challenges, skills, and change readiness of the organization. Selecting the Lean tools required to support the appropriate performance objectives, guide problem solving, and define specific information needs will vary by level and unit. The Lean practitioner should guide the use of tools as the organization knowledge and skills develop. In general, for most parts of an organization, this effort will start simply and become more advanced over time. It will also vary by level and function. For example:

- Front-line operations will tend to focus on improving the cost, quality, or timeliness of products and services.
- Staff functions will tend to work on aligning their activities to increase the value of products or services through joint efforts with front-line operations.
- Management groups will tend to concentrate on identifying the most attractive performance improvement opportunities and on designing the processes to exploit them.

What is important in your planning efforts is that they are:

- *Focused.* Organizations most often perform well with less than perfect strategies, but not with unclear objectives. For leaders of the Lean Transformation it is at times easy to focus attention on organizational culture away from tangible performance goals. But this puts things the wrong way around. The best way to a Lean culture is to define and reinforce the required behaviors to improve performance.
- *Integrated.* All four axes are worked simultaneously in a way that is mutually reinforcing and drives core business performance. At the same time plans need to create room for innovation required to address changing customer and technological challenges.
- *Resourced.* Explicit attention must also be given to the relative emphasis paid to each axis. This does not mean equal efforts and resources applied to each axis as this may be the wrong formula. We suggest balancing resources to the opportunities appropriate for achieving the specific company objectives.
- *Team-based.* Teams are critical for all four axes.
  - Top-down activities—it is essential to build a leadership team to integrate initiatives and create the leader standard work to lead the process;
  - Bottom-up Improvement actions—there will ultimately be multiple performance-improvement teams working to apply Lean concepts in every part of the organization;
  - Cross-functional redesign efforts—value stream management teams have to come together across direct and supporting functions.

– Customer and Technology Shifts—Cross-functional Teams including customers, suppliers, outside thought leaders have to come together across industries.

Flexibility Is Required

Finally it may be comforting to have all the answers written in a book that fits in one's pocket; however, the world in which we live today is mind-blowingly complex, and not only does it insist on increasing in complexity, but the rate of that increase is skyrocketing. The only way to survive is to be capable of adapting and changing as you progress. It is in this environment we work to create our business transformation plans. Continual transformation is like sailing. When winds change, you have to adjust your sails. Sometimes when the winds change, you have to change sails. Other times when the winds change, you have to change destinations. This is what continual Lean transformation is all about, being open and inclusive enough to plan a course and flexible enough to make adjustments and then act on them.

Here is a deep thought we would like to leave you with:

> Excellence is an art won by training and habituation. We do not act rightly because we have virtue or excellence, but we rather have those because we have acted rightly. We are what we repeatedly do. Excellence, then, is not an act but a habit.
>
> **—Aristotle**

Checklists

Understanding the risks of change, we have created checklists for implementing and sustaining Lean for the three major stakeholder groups who make things happen. There will be new questions that emerge in the future, but these should put the reader on the trail. Our intention is to guide the readers' thoughts toward learning and continuous improvement in the process of developing Lean for the long term to achieve excellence.

Checklist for Building Your Plan: Lean Practitioner

1. Identify and adopt a management support mentor.
2. Gain in-depth training in Lean tools and principles.

3. Understand the business model.
4. Understand the customers/customer value.
5. Understand the company Lean approach.
6. Volunteer to plot the value stream to understand enterprise opportunities.
7. Work big opportunities for impact and visibility.
8. Help management create a Lean management system.
9. Mentor workers around you to build capability.

Checklist for Building Your Plan: Upper Management

1. Study management approaches and understand the value of Lean across the enterprise. (This book should help.)
2. Adopt Lean as an overall strategy for the company.
3. Construct a Lean management system that actively involves all functions.
4. Use Lean practitioners to analyze the business model, growth opportunities, and innovation experiments.
5. Continually communicate to all stakeholders that the company is on the Lean journey without question.
6. Plan for Lean to be a 30+-year journey.
7. Manage Lean maturity to see it move through phases 1, 2, and 3.
8. See that management is trained first and has jobs to train and mentor others.
9. Work to create a succession plan for all upper management that includes Lean as a requirement.
10. Create management standard work that is both visible and valuable in all departments.
11. Celebrate successes and learning from failures.

Checklist for Building Your Plan: Board of Directors

1. Understand the successes of the Lean long-term leaders and their culture, even in difficult markets.
2. Be in tune with the culture of the company and which way it is headed.
3. Evaluate the staff on their continuous improvement, people involvement, and respect for people efforts continuously and reward them appropriately.
4. When interviewing successors in upper management, require strong Lean leadership.

Appendix: The Original Stocks in the S&P Index

1. Philip Morris
2. Thatcher Glass
3. National Can
4. Dr. Pepper
5. Lane Bryand
6. Warner-Lambert
7. General Foods
8. Abbot labs
9. Celanese
10. Bristol-Myers
11. Columbia Pictures
12. Sweets Co.
13. American Chicle
14. Pfizer
15. Coca-Cola
16. California Packing Corp
17. Merck
18. Lorillard
19. National Dairy Products
20. Standard Brands
21. Richardson Merrell
22. Houdaille Industries
23. Reeves Brothers
24. R.H. Macy
25. Stokely-Van Camp
26. PepsiCo
27. McCall
28. Colgate-Palmolive
29. R.J. Reynolds Industries
30. Crane Co.
31. Consolidated Cigar
32. Penick & Ford
33. Bestfoods
34. Paramount Pictures
35. General Cigars
36. Virginia Carolina Chemical
37. Congoleum-Nairn
38. Truax-Traer Coal
39. American Agricultural Chemical
40. Amalgamated Sugar
41. Heinz
42. Corn Products
43. Wrigley
44. American Tobacco
45. Electric Auto-Lite
46. Bohn Aluminum & Brass
47. Flintkote
48. Quaker Oats
49. Gulf Mobile & Ohio RR
50. Kroger
51. Schering
52. Container Corp. of America

53. Procter & Gamble
54. Swift
55. Hershey Foods
56. Norwich Pharmacal
57. American Broadcasting Co.
58. Storer Broadcasting
59. Royal Crown Cola
60. Spiegel
61. Wesson Oil
62. Howmet
63. American Home Products
64. Chicago Pneumatic Tool
65. Safeway Stores
66. C.I.T. Financial
67. Merganthaler Linotype
68. Elliot Co.
69. Sunshine Biscuits
70. Columbia Broadcasting
71. Royal Dutch Petroleum
72. Mohasco Industries
73. Texas Gulf Sulphur
74. Amstar
75. General Mills
76. Beechnut Life Saver
77. McGraw-Hill
78. Consolidation Coal
79. Dixie Cup
80. Melville Shoe
81. Magnavox
82. Kayser Roth
83. Worthington
84. National Buscuit
85. Marathon
86. Amsted Industries
87. Shell Oil
88. Masonite
89. Canada Dry
90. Socony Vacuum Oil
91. Beatrice Foods
92. Motorola
93. American Can
94. Daystrom Inc.
95. Hall Printing
96. North American Aviation
97. Cannon Mills
98. RCA
99. Parke Davis
100. Miami Cooper
101. Equitable Gas
102. Cream of Wheat
103. Standard Oil of Indiana
104. Bayuk Cigars
105. Associated Dry Goods
106. Borg Warner
107. ACF industries
108. Deere
109. United Electric Coal
110. Household Finance
111. Rockwell Standard
112. Pitney Bowes
113. Kimberly-Clark
114. Otis Elevator
115. Twentieth-Century-Fox
116. Tidewater Oil
117. ArcherDaniels-Midland
118. Spencer Kellogg
119. American Standard
120. Standard Oil of New Jersey
121. Beneficial
122. Columbian Carbon
123. Eaton
124. Consolidated Natural Gas
125. American Brake Shoe
126. Bliss EW
127. Cutler-Hammer
128. Montgomery Ward
129. Southern Pacific

130. Minnesota Mining & Manufacturing
131. Marshall Field
132. National Gypsum
133. Continental Oil
134. Boeing
135. Admiral
136. Martin-Marietta
137. Yale & Towne
138. General Electric
139. Associates Investments
140. Crucible Steel
141. Gulf Oil
142. Denver Rio Grande
143. American Crystal Sugar
144. Atlantic Richfield
145. Continental Can
146. St. Louis-San Francisco
147. Illinois Central RR
148. Gimbel Brothers
149. Westinhouse Air Brake
150. American Stores
151. Pullman
152. Square D
153. Beckman Instruments
154. International Business Machines
155. South Puerto Rico Sugar
156. United Aircraft
157. Firth Carpet
158. Monsanto Chemical
159. Scovill Manufacturing
160. Raytheon
161. Armour Co.
162. Condé Naste
163. Mack Truck
164. Consolidated Edison
165. Schenley Industries
166. Laclede Gas
167. International Telephone & Telegraph
168. Texas Gulf Producing
169. Foremost Dairies
170. Ford Motor
171. Studebaker Packard
172. Moore McCormack Resources
173. Standard Oil of California
174. American Cyanamid
175. Brooklyn Union Gas
176. Campbell Soup
177. Ruberoid
178. American Enka
179. Bath Iron Works
180. Clevite Corp.
181. Peoples Gas Light Coke
182. Diamond T Motor Car
183. Cooper Industries
184. Crown Cork & Seal
185. Florida Power
186. Bendix
187. Atchison, Topeka, Santa Fe
188. Sears Roebuck
189. Cities Service
190. Oklahoma Natural Gas
191. Mercantile Stores
192. Southern Railway
193. Gardner-Denver
194. Emerson Radio & Phonograph
195. Federal Paper Board
196. Missouri Pacific
197. May Department Stores
198. Intertype
199. Peninsular Telephone
200. Jacob Ruppert
201. Texas Pacific Coal & Oil
202. Continental Baking
203. Washington Gas Light
204. Harris Seybold

205. Southern
206. New England Electric System
207. Pittsburgh Plate Glass
208. Liggett Group
209. Combustion Engineering
210. Texas Co.
211. Baltimore Gas & Electric
212. Alco Products
213. Public Service Electric and Gas
214. Dayton Power & Light
215. Olin
216. Philco
217. Seaboard Oil
218. Cincinnati Gas & Electric
219. Phillips Petroleum
220. Celotex
221. Union Pacific Railroad
222. Philadelphia Electric
223. Cuneo Press
224. Servel
225. Smith-Douglass
226. Virgina Electric
227. General Telephone & Electric
228. Sylvania Electric Products
229. Union Oil of California
230. Dow Chemical
231. Freeport Sulphur
232. General Dynamics
233. Great Northern
234. New York, Chicago & St. Louis
235. Caterpillar Tractor Inc.
236. Grand Union
237. United Biscuit of America
238. American Telephone & Telegraph
239. Wayne Pump
240. McGraw Edison
241. Sinclair Oil
242. Mississipp River

243. Brown Group
244. Northern Pacific
245. St. Joseph Lead
246. American Natural Gas
247. Middle South Utilities
248. New York State Electric & Gas
249. Dome Mines
250. Magma Copper
251. Southern California Edison
252. Union Bag Camp Paper
253. Jewel Tea
254. Waukesha Motors
255. Pacific Telephone & Telegraph
256. Union Carbide & Carbon
257. Beaunit
258. Lerner Stores
259. Deleware Power & Light
260. Fajardo Sugar
261. Northern States Power Minn.
262. General Signal
263. Sterling Drug
264. Lockheed Aircraft
265. Commonwealth Edison
266. Panhandle Eastern
267. Reliance Manufacturing
268. Ingersoll-Rand
269. Kennecott Copper
270. International Minerals & Chemicals
271. Winn-Dixie Stores
272. Air Reduction
273. Endicott Johnson
274. Borden
275. Scott Paper
276. Louisville & Nashville
277. Centeral & South West
278. Dana
279. United States Lines
280. Industrial Rayon

281. Bond Stores
282. Detriot Edison
283. CNW (Chicago & North Western)
284. Clark Equipment
285. Central Aguirre Sugar
286. Mead
287. Pacific Gas & Electric
288. United Gas
289. Cerro De Pasco
290. Columbia Gas System
291. McCrory Stores
292. Atlantic Coast Line
293. Becor Western
294. United States Gypsum
295. Chesapeake & Ohio Railway
296. St. Regis
297. Westinghouse Electric
298. Seaboard Finance
299. National Sugar Refining
300. Halliburton
301. United States Rubber
302. Anaconda Copper Mining
303. Acme Cleveland
304. Curtis Publishing
305. Thompson Products
306. Libbey-Owens-Ford
307. General Cable
308. Westvaco Corp.
309. Cleveland Elec. Illuminating
310. General Public Utilities
311. American Gas & Electric
312. Divco Wayne
313. Pacific Enterprises
314. Curtiss-Wright
315. Lowenstein & Sons
316. McIntyre Porcupine
317. Chicago Milwaukee St. Paul Pacific
318. National Cash Register
319. Duquesne Light
320. West Penn Electric
321. Link Belt
322. DWG Cigars
323. Cuban American Sugar
324. W. R. Grace
325. American Zinc Lead & Smelting
326. Dresser Industries
327. American Machine & Foundry
328. J.C. Penney
329. E.I. DuPont de Nemours
330. General Motors
331. National Dist. & Chem
332. Owens Illinios Glass
333. Ward Baking
334. H.L. Green
335. Bridgeport Brass
336. F.W. Woolworth
337. Corning Glassworks
338. El Paso Natural Gas
339. Marquette Cement Manufacturing
340. Sutherland Paper
341. Aluminum Company of America
342. Phelps Dodge
343. Bullard Co.
344. Blaw Knox
345. Universal Pictures
346. Eastman Kodak
347. Texas Utilities
348. American Bakeries
349. Chrysler
350. Libby, McNeill & Libby
351. Commercial Solvents
352. General Portland Cement
353. National Lead
354. International Paper
355. Jefferson Lake Sulphur

356. Douglas Aircraft
357. Allied Chemical & Dye
358. Lilly Tulip
359. Indianapolis Power & Light
360. Climax Molybdenum
361. Anaconda Wire & Cable
362. Firestone Tire & Rubber
363. Baltimore & Ohio
364. Island Creek Coal
365. Newport News Shipbuilding
366. American Metal Climax
367. Chicago R.I. & Pacific
368. Niagara Mohawk Power
369. Oliver
370. Dayton Rubber
371. General Finance
372. National Tea
373. Aluminum
374. Homestake Mining
375. Champion Power
376. Hercules Motors
377. Reed Roller Bit
378. Walker Hiram Goooderham & Worts
379. Southern Natural Gas
380. American Chain & Cable
381. First National Stores
382. Lehigh Portland Cement
383. Revere Copper & Brass
384. J.J. Newberry
385. Erie Railroad
386. General Host
387. Reynolds Metal
388. Hercules Powder
389. Cudahy Packing
390. Chain Belt Co.
391. Royal McBee
392. Fruehauf Trailer Corp.
393. Falstaff Brewing
394. Amerada Petroleum
395. Burroughs
396. Crown Zellerbach
397. American Motors
398. Goodrich
399. Briggs Manufacturing
400. American Airlines
401. Alpha Portland Industries
402. Illinois Power
403. American Smetling & Refining
404. Babcock & Wilcox
405. Case (Ji)
406. Enserch
407. International Nickel Co. CDA
408. U S Steel
409. Copper Range
410. Goodyear Tire & Rubber
411. Republic Aviation
412. Bigelow-Sanford
413. Sperry Rand
414. Distillers Corp Seagram
415. Motor Wheel
416. Cincinnati Milling Machine
417. Consumers Power
418. Great Western Sugar
419. Commercial Credit
420. Foster Wheeler
421. Diana Stores
422. Vanadium
423. Walworth Co.
424. Dan River
425. Pfeiffer Brewing
426. Inland Street
427. Munsingwear
428. Genesco
429. Pen-Dixie Industries
430. Kaiser Aluminum
431. Missouri-Kansas-Texas
432. United Airlines

433. Allied Supermarkets
434. Armstrong Cork
435. Inspiration Consolidated Copper
436. Interantional Harvester
437. Lone Star Industries
438. S.H. Kress
439. Kresge
440. National Supply
441. Armco Steel
442. Allied Stores
443. Owens Corning
444. Federated Department Stores
445. American Viscose
446. Penn Central
447. Manville
448. Cone Mills
449. New York Central
450. Holland Furnace
451. Nothern Natural Gas
452. Food Fair Stores
453. Van Raalte
454. Stevens (JP)
455. Aldens Inc.
456. Cluett Peabody
457. Trans World Airlines
458. Jones & Laughlin Steel
459. American Export Lines
460. Lees & Sons
461. Youngstown Sheet & Tube
462. Warner Brothers
463. Wilson Co.
464. Burlington Industries
465. Allis Chalmers
466. Reading Co.
467. Publicker Industries

468. Family Finance
469. Wheeling Steel Corp.
470. Republic Pictures
471. Bethlehem Steel
472. Addressograph Multigraph
473. American Shipbuilding
474. Colorado Fuel & Iron
475. Cornell-Dubilier
476. Eagle Picher
477. Eastern Airlines
478. Goebel Brewing
479. W.T. Grant
480. Guantanamo Sugar
481. Holly Sugar
482. International Shoe
483. Jaeger Machine
484. Joy Manufacturing
485. Manati Sugar
486. Manhattan Shirt
487. Monarch Machine Tool
488. Minneapolis Moline
489. G.C. Murphy
490. National Steel
491. New York, New Haven & Hartford
492. Pan American World Airways
493. Republic Steel
494. Sunbeam
495. Artloom Carpet
496. U.S. Hoffman Machinery
497. United States Smelting and Refining
498. Vertientes-Camaguey Sugar
499. White Motors
500. Zenith Radio

Index

About the Authors

Bill Baker has been a frequent speaker at Speed To Excellence on benchmarking, performance measurement, knowledge management, Raytheon Six Sigma, and the Lean Enterprise. He has been instrumental in assisting several companies and organizations pursue their strategic objectives, including Raytheon, Texas Instruments, Northrop Grumman, Sandia, Kirtland AFB, ESCO, AME, APQC, U.S. Air Force, U.S. Army, ASQ, and the Shingo Prize.

Mr. Baker is a senior Shingo Prize examiner and was a key design contributor to the Lean certification process developed by AME-Shingo-SME and launched in 2006.

He was responsible for knowledge management, benchmarking, and the benchmarking process at both Texas Instruments and Raytheon from 1990 until 2004. He trained and conducted numerous benchmarking teams and projects, ranging from strategic to tactical focus. He led the Raytheon effort to benchmark Six Sigma strategies, including site visits to GE and Allied Signal. Under his leadership and planning Raytheon received the MAKE (Most Admired Knowledge Enterprise) Finalist designation in the United States by Teleos in 2003 and was the North American winner in 2004, 2005, and 2006.

Earlier in his career he was the manufacturing manager on several high-profile missile/electronic systems, including Shrike, Paveway, Harpoon Seeker, TOW Night Sight, HARM, and Tacit Rainbow, as well as the Lunar Mass Spectrometer experiments on Apollo 15, 16, and 17. He was the U.S. Air Force engineering chief, responsible for evaluating satellite launches at Vandenberg AFB, California.

He has contributed articles to the *National Productivity Review*, *Target*, and *Quality Progress*, and his work has been featured in numerous books.

He is referenced in *The Complete Idiot's Guide to Knowledge Management* and *The Knowledge Evolution*. With Michael English in 2006 he coauthored the best-selling book *Winning the Knowledge Transfer Race*, published by McGraw-Hill.

In 2012 he was selected to serve as the chairman of the AME *Target* magazine's editorial board, coordinating the ideas of nine highly qualified experts to improve the publication.

Ken Rolfes, president of KDR Associates, Inc. works with his customers to develop business performance improvement programs on a focused or enterprise-wide basis for service and manufacturing companies. He helps businesses craft and execute winning value creation and growth agendas that maximize the value of the business to its customers, employees, and shareholders.

Ken has more than 35 years senior operations management experience for public and private companies. He served as COO and VP in mid-cap and start-up companies and held key management positions in product management, manufacturing, supply chain management, and quality assurance for NCR and Control Data. He has worked extensively with businesses that design, manufacture, and market technically based products for the medical device, industrial product, and computer industries and has guided organizations in aerospace, military, manufacturing, retail, and service industries.

Ken holds a BS in industrial engineering and a MBA in finance. He has presented at various industry and AME national conferences and at workshops, acted as contributing editor for *Modern Woodworking* magazine, and served as an instructor for San Diego State University in the Lean Enterprise Program. Ken currently serves as director of the Association for Manufacturing Excellence (AME).